SCENOGRAPHY IN CANADA
■ SELECTED DESIGNERS

NATALIE REWA

UNIVERSITY OF TORONTO PRESS

Toronto Buffalo London

© University of Toronto Press Incorporated 2004
Toronto Buffalo London
Printed in Canada

ISBN 0-8020-0685-x (cloth)
ISBN 0-8020-8554-7 (paper)

Printed on acid-free paper

National Library of Canada Cataloguing in Publication

Rewa, Natalie, 1956–
  Scenography in Canada : selected designers / Natalie Rewa.

  Includes bibliographical references and index.
  ISBN 0-8020-0685-x (bound).   ISBN 0-8020-8554-7 (pbk.)

  1. Set designers – Canada.   2. Theaters – Stage-setting and scenery –
  Canada   I. Title.

  PN2087.C3R49 2004   792'.025'092271   C2003-903524-7

University of Toronto Press acknowledges the financial assistance to its publishing program of the Canada Council
for the Arts and the Ontario Arts Council.

University of Toronto Press acknowledges the financial support for its publishing activities of the Government of
Canada through the Book Publishing Industry Development Program (BPIDP).

For MJS

CONTENTS

ACKNOWLEDGMENTS

Among the highly significant changes in the making of theatre in Canada since the late 1960s some of the most exciting have been developments in scenographic design. The number of theatre companies and venues has grown exponentially in the past forty years and with this expansion opportunities for designers to work in diverse kinds of theatres have opened up. Their designs have been realized in all manner of architectural setting, from renovated vaudeville and opera houses, to multi-theatre civic arts centres, to the post-industrial spaces reclaimed for performance.

This book is an attempt to bring the discussion of scenography to the forefront, and to the draw the reader into the imaginations of artists. Without the full cooperation of the artists whose work is included the project would have been impossible. From the initial letter of inquiry each one of these artists has been wonderfully generous in answering questions leading to more questions in the midst of the pressures of their current work. Access to their personal archives has allowed me to study what happens in the studio, as well as what we as spectators see in performance. For their unstinting support and kindness I warmly thank Susan Benson, Astrid Janson, Mary Kerr, Michael Levine, Ken MacDonald, Jim Plaxton, and Teresa Przybylski.

While the commentary about scenographic design may be relatively recent, the interest in theatre designs is not. Special tribute is due to Heather McCallum, who as the prescient Head of Theatre Department of the Toronto Reference Library started its distinguished collection of costume and set sketches, and to Lee Ramsay, the current Head of the Arts Department who continues to build the collection with energy and acumen. The Special Collections at the Toronto Reference Library and the expertise of curator Anne Sutherland and other staff members have been invaluable resources for this book. Other archives have also been productive and I particularly thank those who

have made them accessible for me: Bernard Katz and his staff at the Archives in the McLaughlin Library at the University of Guelph; Lisa Brant and later Jane Edmonds of the Stratford Archives; Lee Milliken and Mark Zurowski of the Production Department of the Canadian Opera Company; Greg Parry of the Banff Centre for the Arts; Clare Seed of the English National Opera Company; Sharon Vanderlinde of the National Ballet of Canada; Nicola Woods of the Royal Ontario Museum; Jonathan Tichler of the Metropolitan Opera in New York.

For financial support my thanks are especially due to the Woodlawn Foundation whose support of the publication of materials about theatre in Canada has made this publication possible. Thanks are due also to the Academic Research Council of Queen's University, which has supported my research confidently and generously, and the Office of Research Services, which has supported the publication of this research.

I am especially grateful to Suzanne Rancourt of the University of Toronto Press, whose patience and commitment to the project have been so consistent, and to the design and editorial staff.

On a personal level, I offer heartfelt thanks to Tetiana Rewa, whose passion for theatre, opera, and ballet I have come to share. For his continuing intellectual support, sense of equilibrium, encouragement, and love I thank Michael J. Sidnell.

PORTFOLIOS

The illustrations are intended to convey some sense of the artistic processes and excitement of scenographic design, not just to show finished stage settings. As designers conceive of a three-dimensional theatrical space for actors, they also develop a visual narrative for the spectators. The maquettes, sketches, excerpts from notebooks, and production photos are traces of this dynamic scenographic creation. Each designer demonstrates an idiosyncratic approach to *seeing* the evolution of the scenography, so the documents that chart their process are varied and are presented to emphasize the diversity of approaches. The photos have been organized by designer, but the reader is encouraged to provide her or his own entrée into the study of scenography as they look at drawings or elements of design. These photos are matched to the subsequent chapters concerning specific designers.

1

2

3

4

5

6

7

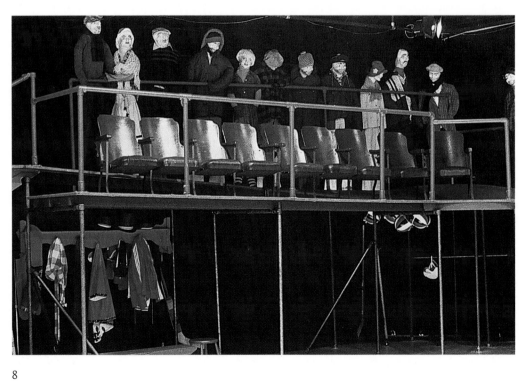

8

9

10

11

12

13

14

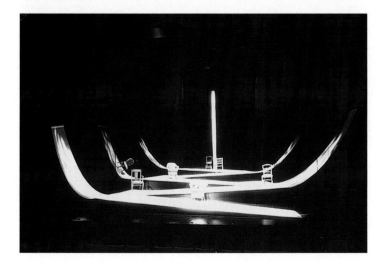

15

16

17

18

19

20

21

22

23

24

25

26

27

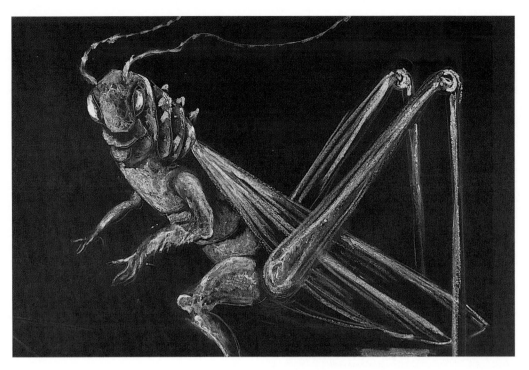

28

29

30

31

32

33

34

35

36

37

38

39

40

41

42

43

44

45

46

47

48

49

50

51

52

53

54

55

56

57

58

59

60

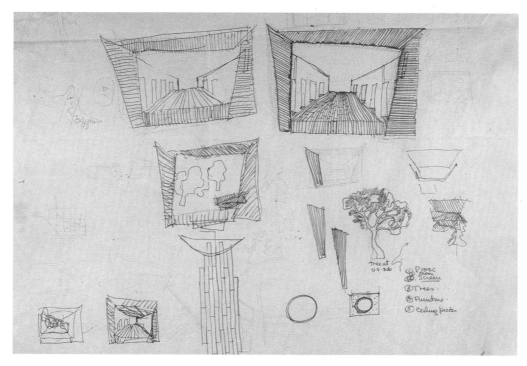

61

62

63

64

65

66

67

68

69

70

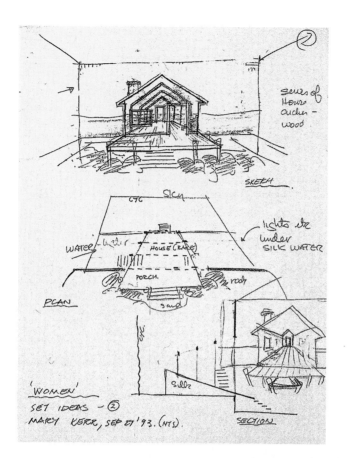

71

72

73

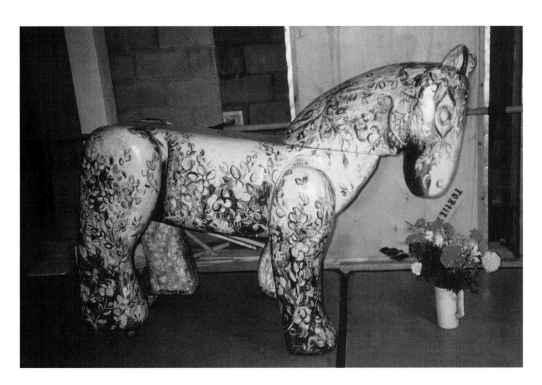

74

75

76

77

78

79

80

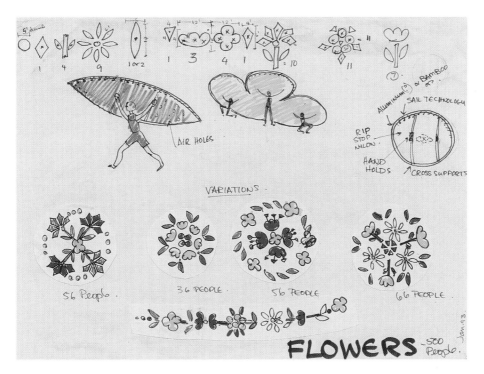

81

82

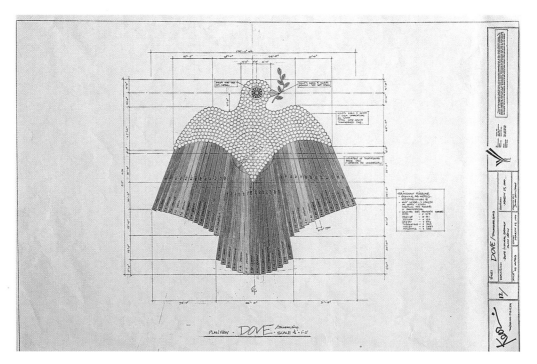

83

84

85

86

87

88

89

90

91

92

93

94

95

96

97

98

99

100

101

102

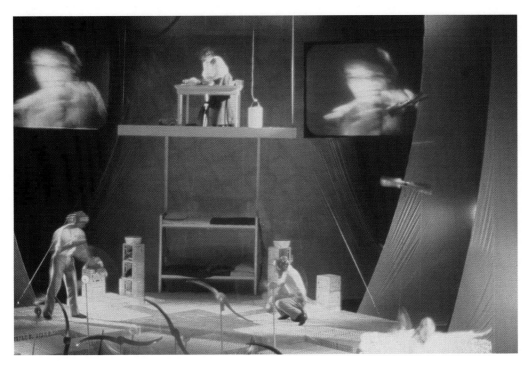

103

104

105

106

107

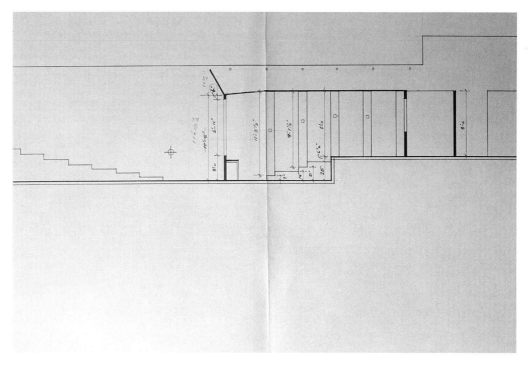

108

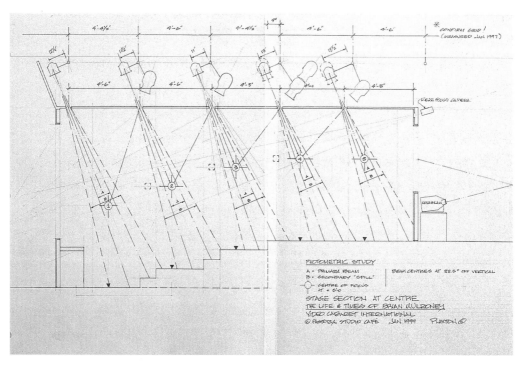

109

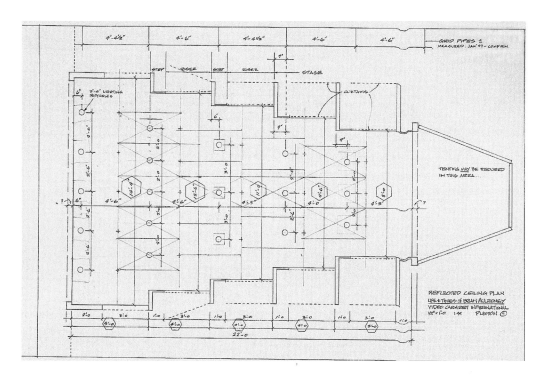

110

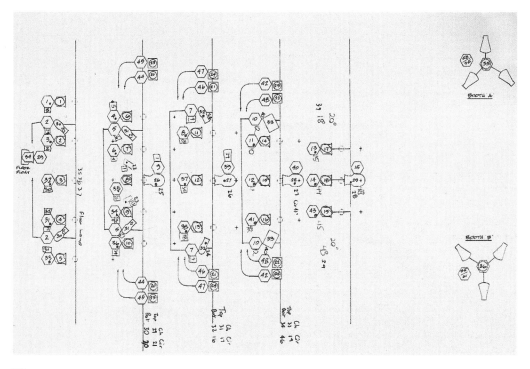

111

112

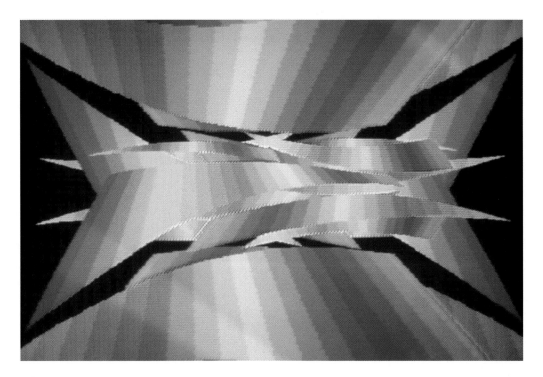

113

114

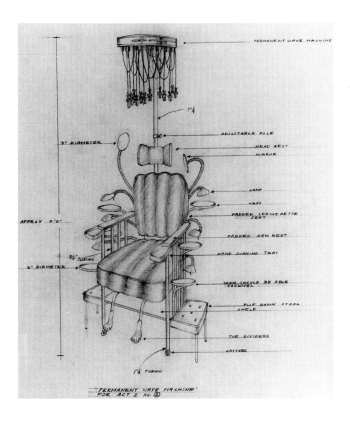

115

116

117

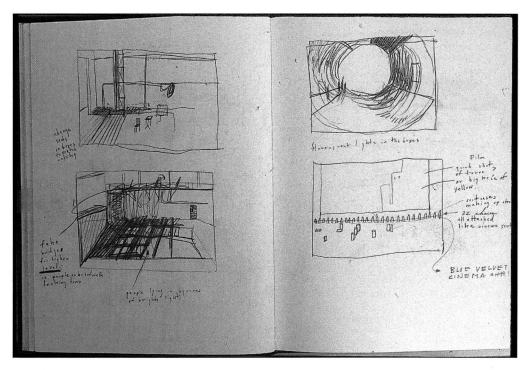

118

119

120

121

122

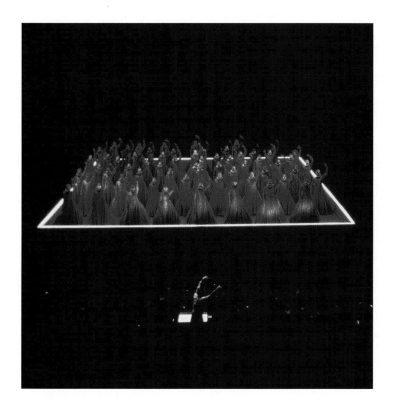

123

124

125

126

127

128

129

130

131

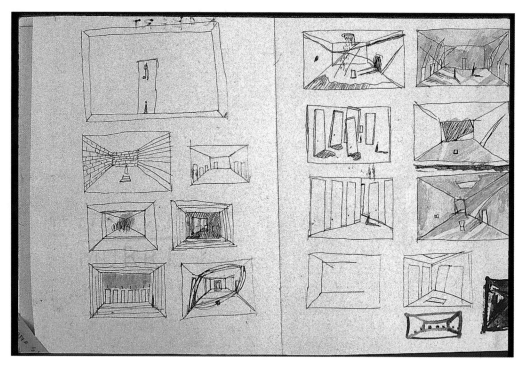

132

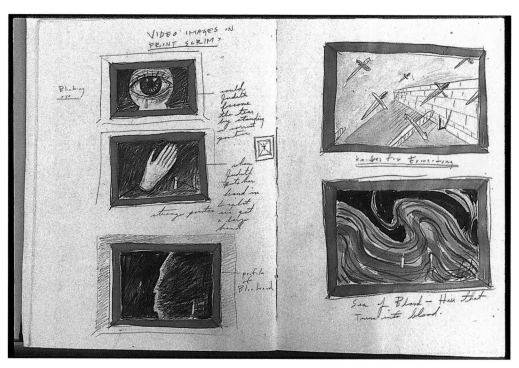

133

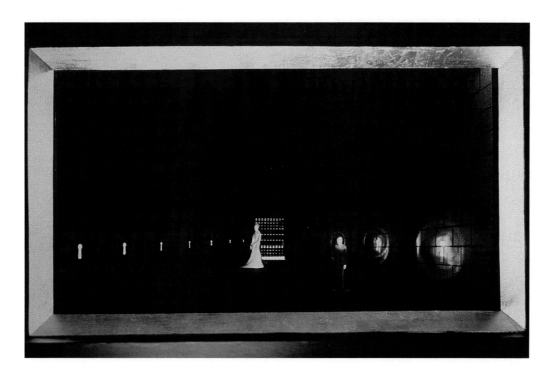

134

135

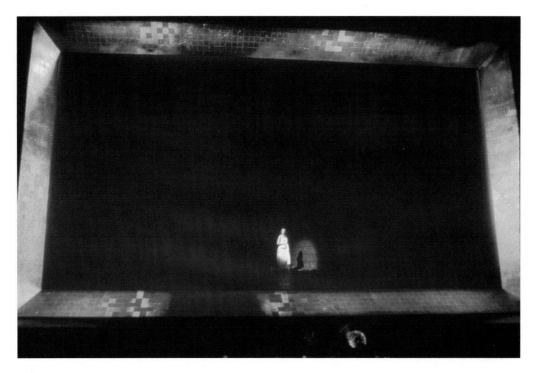

136

137

138

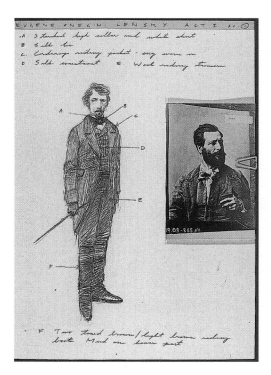

139

140

141

142

143

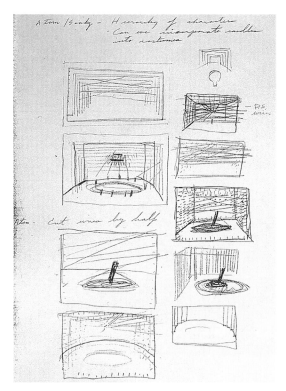

144

145

146

147

148

149

150

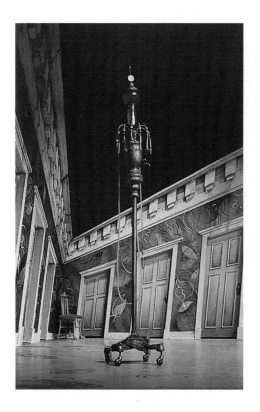

151

152

153

154

155

156

157

158

159

160

161

162

163

164

165

166

167

168

169

170

171

172

173

174

175

176

177

178

179

180

181

182

183

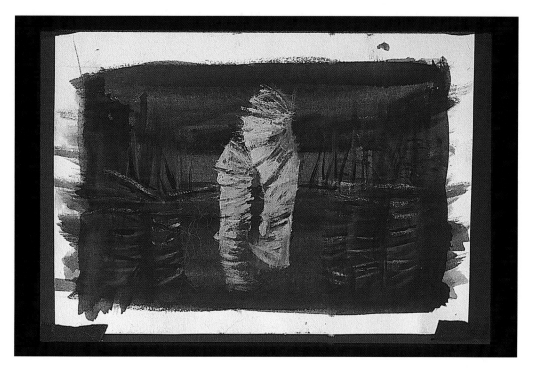

184

185

186

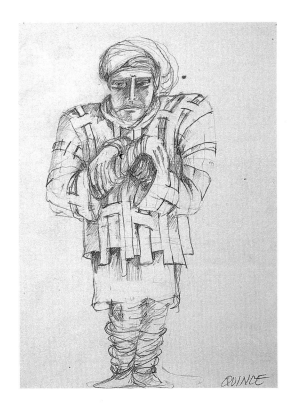

187

188

189

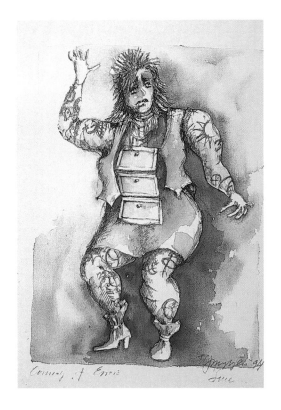

Company of Errors
Jame

190

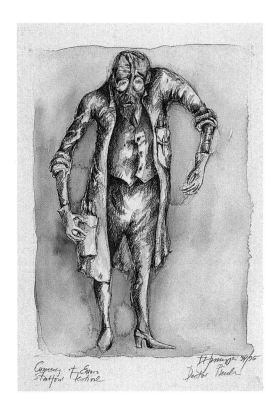

Company of Errors
Stratford Festival
Doctor Pinch

191

192

193

194

195

Emperor of Atlantis. C.O.C. Last Scene S.S. ?Krzywicki 77

196

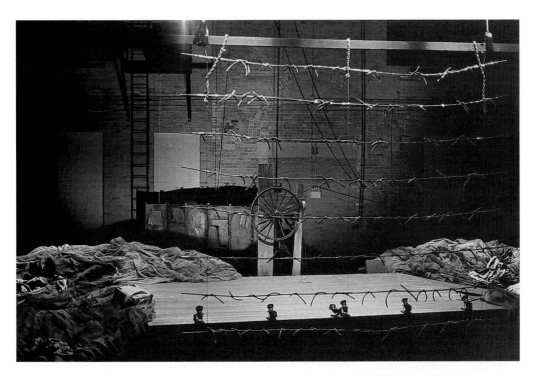

197

198

199

200

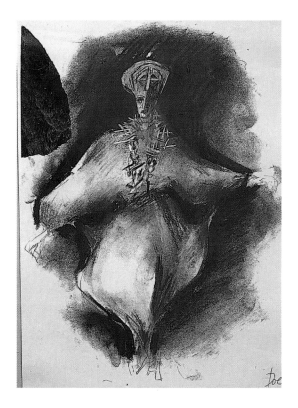

201

202

203

204

205

206

207

PORTFOLIO CAPTIONS

ASTRID JANSON

Charming and Rose by Kelley Jo Burke
Directed by Kate Lushington
Nightwood Theatre, Theatre Centre, 1993

1 Stage: The room in the tower
Photo: David Cooper

Woman in Mind by Alan Ayckbourn
Directed by Martha Henry
Grand Theatre, London, 1991

2 Stage: The garden in full growth
Photo: Robert C. Ragsdale

Passion by Stephen Sondheim
Directed by Jordan Merkur
Co-production by Eclectic Theatre, Tapestry
   Theatre, and Canadian Stage Theatre in
   the Bluma Appel Theatre, 1997

3 Act II, scene 3: The castle garden
Photo: Nir Bareket
4 Scene 7: Fosca's bedroom: Fosca (Mary
   Ann McDonald) and Giorgio (Curtis
   Sullivan)
Photo: Nir Bareket

You Can't Get Here from There by Jack Winter
Directed by George Luscombe
Toronto Workshop Productions, 1974–5

5 Scene from a performance with the
   doors of the cube open
Photo: Robert C. Ragsdale
6 Scene from a performance with the
   doors of the cube closed
Photo: Robert C. Ragsdale

Les Canadiens by Rick Salutin with an assist
   by Ken Dryden
Directed by George Luscombe
Toronto Workshop Productions, 1977

7 The rink with ramps
Photo: Robert C. Ragsdale
8 The rink with seats for the audience,
   with the 'fans' standing behind them
Photo: Robert C. Ragsdale

Village of the Small Huts VI: The Great War by
   Michael Hollingsworth
Directed by Michael Hollingsworth
Theatre Centre, Toronto, 1992

9 Act 1, scene 43: Duchess of Connaught
   (Janet Burke) and Duke of Connaught,
   Governor General of Canada (Hugo
   Dann)
Photo: J. Hovey
10 Act 2, scene, 19: At the front lines
   British General Byng confers with
   Canadian General Currie.

From L to R: Soldiers (Janet Burke and
   Cliff Saunders), Byng (John Blackwood),
   Currie (Alan Bridle), and Soldier (Hugo
   Dann)
   Photo: J. Hovey

*Village of the Small Huts VII: The Life and Times
of Mackenzie King* by Michael
   Hollingsworth
Theatre Centre, Toronto, 1993

11 Act 2, scene 47: The election of 1935:
     Mackenzie King (Layne Coleman) with
     R.B. Bennett (Edward Roy)
     Photo: Michael Cooper

The Cold War by Michael Hollingsworth
Directed by Michael Hollingsworth
Theatre Centre, Toronto, 1995

12 The family: Tommy Muffet, Jr. (Dave
     Carley), Mary Muffet (Janet Burke),
     Tommy Muffet (Layne Coleman), and
     Nancy Muffet (Beverly Cooper)
     Photo: Michael Cooper

Molly Sweeney by Brian Friel
Directed by Miles Potter
Co-production by Grand Theatre, London,
   and Canadian Stage Company in the
   Bluma Appel Theatre, 1998

13–15 Transformation of the stage
     Photos: Michael Cooper

The Cherry Orchard by Anton Chekhov
Directed by Radu Penciulescu
Festival Theatre, Shaw Festival, 1980

16 Act II
     Photo: David Cooper
17 Act IV: Lopakhin (Terence Kelly) and
     Varya (Deborah Kipp)
     Photo: David Cooper

The Cherry Orchard by Anton Chekhov
Directed by Diana Leblanc
Tom Patterson Theatre, Stratford Festival,
   1998

18 Act II
     Stratford Festival Archives
     Photo: Cylla von Tiedemann
19 Act III
     Stratford Festival Archives
     Photo: Cylla von Tiedemann

Reflections at Expo '86 (Vancouver)
Installation by Astrid Janson
Vancouver, 1986

20 The fight for the colony between the
     French and the English
     Private collection Astrid Janson
     Photo: Barrie Jones
21 Confederation Follies
     Private collection Astrid Janson
     Photo: Barrie Jones
22 Maquette for Modern Ontario
     Private collection Astrid Janson
     Photo: Barrie Jones

Discovery Gallery, Royal Ontario Museum,
   1998

23 Discovery Gallery – scale model
     Photo: Royal Ontario Museum

The Glass Menagerie by Tennessee Williams
Directed by Diana Leblanc
Tarragon Theatre, 1998

24 Costume sketch: Amanda and Laura
     Private collection Astrid Janson
25 Scrim walls on the stage
     Photo: Nir Bareket

Long Day's Journey into Night by Eugene
    O'Neill
Directed by Diana Leblanc
Tom Patterson Theatre, Stratford Festival,
    1994, 1995

26 Costume sketch: Mary Tyrone, Act 2
    Private collection Astrid Janson

Rusalka by Anton Dvořák
Directed by Gray Veredun
Opera Company of Philadelphia, 1988

27 Costume sketch: Water sprites
    Private collection Astrid Janson

Incognito choreography by Robert
    Desrosiers
Calgary Olympics, 1998

28 Costume sketch: Insect
    Private collection Astrid Janson

SUSAN BENSON

A Midsummer Night's Dream by William
    Shakespeare
Directed by Robin Phillips
Festival Theatre, Stratford Festival, 1976

29 The court
    Stratford Festival Archives
    Photo: Robert C. Ragsdale
30 Jessica Tandy as Titania and Jeremy
    Brett as Oberon
    Stratford Festival Archives
    Photo: Robert C. Ragsdale
31 Costume sketch: Jessica Tandy as
    Titania
    Private collection
32 Costume sketch: Dorian Clark as
    Starveling
    Susan Benson Collection

A Midsummer Night's Dream by William
    Shakespeare
Directed by Robin Phillips
Festival Theatre, Stratford Festival, 1977

33 Costume sketch: Maggie Smith as
    Hippolyta
    Susan Benson Collection
34 Maggie Smith as Titania
    Stratford Festival Archives
    Photo: Robert C. Ragsdale

The Woman by Edward Bond
Directed by Urjo Kareda and Peter Moss
Avon Theatre, Stratford Festival, 1979

35 Costume sketch: Martha Henry as
    Hecuba
    Private collection Susan Benson

Cabaret by Joe Masteroff and Fred Ebb,
    with music by John Kander
Directed by Brian Macdonald
Festival Theatre, Stratford Festival, 1987

36 Costume sketch: Anne Wright as
    Telephone Girl
    Private collection Susan Benson
37 Act 1: Fruitshop guests
    Stratford Festival Archives
    Photo: Michael Cooper

Guys and Dolls by Abe Burrows and Joe
    Swerling, with music by Frank Loesser
Directed by Brian Macdonald
Festival Theatre, Stratford Festival, 1991

38 The finale
    Stratford Festival Archives
    Photo: David Cooper
39 Stratford stage in process of change
    Stratford Festival Archives
    Photo: Jane Edwards
40 Festival Stage
    Stratford Festival Archives
    Photo: David Cooper

41 Details of upstage wall, Festival Stage
Stratford Festival Archives
Photo: David Cooper

The Mikado by W.S. Gilbert, with music by
Arthur Sullivan
Directed by Brian Macdonald
Avon Theatre, Stratford Festival, 1983

42 Costume sketch: The Mikado
Private collection
43 Pooh-Bah, Pish Tush, and the Gentle-
men of Japan
Stratford Festival Archives
Photo: Robert C. Ragsdale
44 Katisha with Company
Stratford Festival Archives
Photo: Robert C. Ragsdale

Madama Butterfly by Puccini
Directed by Brian Macdonald
Canadian Opera Company, 1990

45 Cio-Cio-San with Geishas
Photo: Tessa Buchan
Private collection Susan Benson
46 Entrance of Cio-Cio-San
Photo: Tessa Buchan
Private collection Susan Benson
47 Costume sketch: Cio-Cio-San (Butterfly)
Private collection

The Marriage of Figaro by Wolfgang
Amadeus Mozart
Directed by Colin Graham
The Banff Festival of the Arts, 1990

48 Act I
Photo: Monte Greenshields
49 Act II
Photo: Monte Greenshields
50 Act III
Photo: Monte Greenshields
51 Act IV
Photo: Monte Greenshields

52 Costume sketch: Countess, Act II
Photo: Monte Greenshields

Romeo and Juliet choreography by John
Cranko
Directed by Reid Anderson
National Ballet of Canada, 1994

53 Act 1, v. Artists of the ballet
Photo: Lydia Pawelak
54 Costume sketch: Juliet
Private collection Susan Benson
55 Balcony set with bridge
Photo: Lydia Pawelak
56 Artists of the ballet
Photo: Lydia Pawelak

MARY KERR

The Stag King by Carlo Gozzi,
adapted by Sheldon Rosen
Directed by Stephen Katz
Tarragon Theatre, 1972

57 Stage curtain and theatre boxes
Private collection Mary Kerr
Photo: Mary Kerr
58 Inner stage and 'sculpture' in a niche
Mary Kerr Collection
Photo: Mary Kerr
59 Costume sketch: Clarissa
Mary Kerr Collection
60 Costume sketch: Derandarte
Private collection Mary Kerr

Nothing Sacred by George F. Walker, based
on *Fathers and Sons* by Ivan Turgenev
Directed by Bill Glassco
Bluma Appel Theatre, St Lawrence Centre,
1988, and a co-production tour by the
National Arts Centre and Citadel
Theatre, 1989

61 Preliminary sketch exploring perspective
Mary Kerr Collection

62 Maquette of set
   Canadian Stage Archives
   Photo: Private collection Mary Kerr
63 Front curtain of birch tree cut-outs
   Photo: Mary Kerr
64 On the estate: Pavel Kirsanov (Richard
   Monette), Bazarov (Robert Bockstael),
   and Arkady (Michael Riley)
   Photo: Nir Bareket
65 Costume sketch: Anna
   Mary Kerr Collection

The Three Penny Opera by Bertolt Brecht,
   with music by Kurt Weill
Directed by Kelly Robinson
Banff Centre for the Arts and Canadian
   Stage, Bluma Appel Theatre,
   St Lawrence Centre, 1989

66 Preliminary sketch for the set
   Mary Kerr Collection
67 Preliminary maquette
   Photo: Mary Kerr Collection
68 Costume sketch: Macheath
   Mary Kerr Collection
69 The stage
   Photo: Michael Cooper
70 Finale
   Photo: Michael Cooper

If We Are Women by Joanna McClelland Glass
Directed by Susan Cox
Co-production Vancouver Playhouse, 1993,
   Canadian Stage, 1994

71 Preliminary sketch for the set #2
   Private collection Mary Kerr
72 Proscenium curtain and set
   Photo: Mary Kerr

73 The set
   Photo: Mary Kerr

Bella Judy Jarvis Dance Company
Choreography Danny Grossman and Judy
   Jarvis
Dance Umbrella, New York City, 1977

74 The horse in the workshop
   Photo: Mary Kerr
75 Costume sketch
   Private collection Mary Kerr
76 Danny Grossman and Judy Jarvis
   Photo: Avrum Fenson

Zurich 1916 by Christopher Butterfield and
   John Bentley Mays
Directed by Keith Turnbull
Banff Centre for the Arts, 1998

77 Costume sketch: 'Parade' horse
   Private collection Mary Kerr
78 Costume sketch: The Tattooed Lady
   Private collection Mary Kerr
79 Costume sketch: Marie and her ponies
   Private collection Mary Kerr
80 Café Voltaire
   Photo: Donald Lee

XV *Commonwealth Games* Opening
   Ceremonies 18 August 1994
Director Jacques Lemay
Victoria, 18 August 1994

81 Sketch: Field formations – Flowers
   Private collection Mary Kerr
82 Wolf puppet
   Private collection Mary Kerr
   Photo: Mary Kerr
83 Design sketch: Dove of peace
   Private collection Mary Kerr
84 Dove of peace
   Private collection Mary Kerr
   Photo: Mary Kerr

JIM PLAXTON

The Crackwalker by Judith Thompson
Directed by Clarke Rogers
Centaur Theatre, 1982

85 Building the set in the Centaur
     Photo: Jim Plaxton
86 Detail: Sandy's apartment
     From L to R: Joe (Frank Moore), Sandy
     (Lynne Deragon), Alan (Hardee T.
     Linehan), Theresa (JoAnn McIntyre)
     Photo: Jim Plaxton
87 Detail: Alan (Hardee T. Linehan) with
     The Man (Graham Greene)
     Photo: Jim Plaxton

O.D. on Paradise by Linda Griffiths and
     Patrick Brymer
Directed by Clarke Rogers
Theatre Passe Muraille, 1984

88 Details of construction: Wooden
     structure for the beach and the
     overhead support for the parachute
     Photo: Jim Plaxton
89 Details of construction: Contours of the
     beach, seen from the balcony, and
     seating for the audience
     Photo: Jim Plaxton
90 Looking at the beach from the lower
     level (rehearsal in progress)
     Photo: Jim Plaxton
91 The expanse of the beach from the
     spectator's view
     Photo: Jim Plaxton

Romeo and Juliet by William Shakespeare
Directed by Guy Sprung
The Dream in High Park, Toronto Free
     Theatre, 1985

92 View of the stage from the hillside
     Photo: Jim Plaxton
93 Detail: Passageway between truck units
     with lighting
     Photo: Jim Plaxton
94 Detail: Integration of the set into the
     natural environment
     Photo: Jim Plaxton
95 Detail: Backstage connections
     Photo: Jim Plaxton

Romeo and Juliet by William Shakespeare
Directed by Guy Sprung
The Dream in High Park, Toronto Free
     Theatre, 1986

96 View of the stage from the hillside
     Photo: Jim Plaxton
97 Detail: The square
     Photo: Jim Plaxton
98 Detail: The balconies
     Photo: Jim Plaxton
99 Detail: Backstage connections
     Photo: Jim Plaxton

Macbeth by William Shakespeare
Directed by Lewis Baumander
Skylight Theatre, Earl Bales Park, 1986

100 View from stage left: The lower stage
      with the upper stage in the distance
      Photo: Jim Plaxton
101 View from stage right: Along the upper
      stage across to the lower stage
      Photo: Jim Plaxton

Hamlet by William Shakespeare
Directed by Graham Harley
Phoenix Theatre, 1981

102 The set
      Photo: Jim Plaxton

Picnic in the Drift by Tanya Mars and Rina
   Fraticelli
Ice House, Harbourfront, 1981

103 The set
     Photo: Jim Plaxton
104 Detail: Podium created from milk
     crates
     Photo: Jim Plaxton
105 Detail: Lighting from the floor
     Photo: Jim Plaxton

History of the Village of the Small Huts and *The
   Global Village* by Michael Hollingsworth
Directed by Michael Hollingsworth
Backspace and Mainspace Theatre Passe
   Muraille, the Theatre Centre, the
   Studio Café at the Factory Theatre,
   1985–98

106 Constructing the first box, Backspace,
     1985
     Photo: Jim Plaxton
107 Testing the lighting, Backspace, 1985
     Photo: Jim Plaxton
108 Side elevation of the box for *Life and
     Times of Brian Mulroney*, 1999
     Plans: Jim Plaxton
109 Photometric study for *Life and Times of
     Brian Mulroney*, 1999
     Plans: Jim Plaxton
110 Reflected ceiling plan for *Life and Times
     of Brian Mulroney*, 1999
     Plans: Jim Plaxton
111 Lighting plot for *Life and Times of Brian
     Mulroney*, 1999
     Plans: Jim Plaxton

Prism, Mirror, Lens choreography by René
   Highway
Toronto Dance Theatre, Native Canadian
   Centre, 1989

112 Slide: 'Prism Mirror Lens' and bear
     Photo: Jim Plaxton
113 Slide: Computer graphics
     Photo: Jim Plaxton

All images and plans from private
collection Jim Plaxton

MICHAEL LEVINE

The Women by Clare Boothe Luce
Directed by Duncan McIntosh
Court House Theatre, 1985, Royal
   Alexandra Theatre, 1987

114 The stage: Mrs Phelps Potter (Robin
     Craig), Dowager (Jillian Cook),
     Mrs John Day (Susan Stackhouse)
     Private collection Michael Levine
     Photo: David Cooper
115 Detail: Permanent wave machine,
     Act 1, scene 2
     Shaw Festival Archives

Heartbreak House by George Bernard
   Shaw
Directed by Christopher Newton
Festival Theatre, Shaw Festival, 1985

116 Act 1: The set (enlarged)
     Shaw Festival Archives
     Photo: David Cooper
117 Act 3: The poop deck looking
     towards the house: Mazzini Dunn
     (Allan Gray), Hesione Hushaby
     (Goldie Semple), and Boss Mangan
     (Robert Benson)
     Shaw Festival Archives
     Photo: David Cooper

Mario and the Magician libretto by Rodney
    Anderson, with music by Harry
    Somers, adapted from the novella by
    Thomas Mann
Directed by Robert Carsen
Canadian Opera Company, Elgin Theatre,
    1992

118 Sketches from the notebook
       Photo: Courtesy of Michael Levine
119 Costume sketch: Stefan
       Michael Levine Collection
120 Act 1: In the lecture hall – maquette
       scale 1:25
       Private collection Michael Levine
       Photo: Michael Cooper
121 Act 1: On the beach – maquette scale
       1:25
       Private collection Michael Levine
       Photo: Michael Cooper
122 Act 2: At the theatre – maquette scale
       1:25
       Private collection Michael Levine
       Photo: Michael Cooper

Rigoletto by Giuseppe Verdi
Directed by Monique Wagemakers
The Netherlands Opera, Amsterdam, 1996

123 Act I
       Private collection Michael Levine
       Photo: Courtesy of Michael Levine
124 Act II
       Private collection Michael Levine
       Photo: Courtesy of Michael Levine
125 Act II
       Private collection Michael Levine
       Photo: Courtesy of Michael Levine

Tectonic Plates by Robert Lepage and
    Théâtre Repère
Directed by Robert Lepage
du Maurier Theatre, Toronto, 1988; tours
    to the Cottesloe Theatre at the
    National Theatre, London; the
    Tramway, Glasgow

126 Sketches from the notebook
       Photo: Courtesy of Michael Levine
127 Sketches from the notebook
       Photo: Courtesy of Michael Levine

Nabucco by Giuseppe Verdi
Directed by Robert Carsen
Bastille Opera, Paris, 1995

128 Maquette scale 1:50
       Photo: Courtesy of Michael Levine
129 Ushering in the new order
       Photo: Michael Levine
130 Detail: Opening of passageways
       Photo: Courtesy of Michael Levine
131 Chorus on the stage
       Photo: Courtesy of Michael Levine

Bluebeard's Castle by Béla Bartók and
    Erwartung by Arnold Schoenberg
Directed by Robert Lepage
Canadian Opera Company, Hummingbird
    Centre, 1993; tours to New York
    (B.A.M.), Edinburgh, Geneva, Mel-
    bourne, and Hong Kong

132 Sketches from the notebook. Set
       design for the double bill
       Photo: Courtesy of Michael Levine
133 Sketches for potential projections on
       the scrim. Left *Bluebeard's Castle,* right
       Erwartung
       Photo: Courtesy of Michael Levine
134 Maquette: *Bluebeard's Castle.* The
       keyholes in the Great Hall – scale 1:25
       Photo: Michael Cooper

135 Maquette: *Bluebeard's Castle*. Light
    flooding through the doors – scale 1:25
    Photo: Michael Cooper
136 Tiled Proscenium opening. The
    Woman (Rebecca Blankenship)
    Photo: Michael Cooper
137 Use of projection on scrim in
    Erwartung: The Psychiatrist (Mark
    Johnson), The Woman (Rebecca
    Blankenship), The Lover (Noam
    Marcus)
    Photo: Michael Cooper

Eugene Onegin by Pyotr Ilyich Tchaikowsky
Directed by Robert Carsen
Metropolitan Opera, New York, 1997

138 Costume sketch: Chorus women
    Act II, scene 1 (ball in St Petersburg)
    Michael Levine Collection
139 Costume sketch: Lensky (Act I,
    scene 1)
    Michael Levine Collection
140 Onegin (Vladimir Chernov) reading
    Tatyana's letter
    Photo: Courtesy of Michael Levine
141 Onegin (Vladimir Chernov) in a winter
    landscape
    Photo: Courtesy of Michael Levine
142 Chorus setting the stage by sweeping
    the leaves into formation
    Photo: Courtesy of Michael Levine
143 The ball in St Petersburg
    Photo: Courtesy of Michael Levine

Dr. Ox's Experiment libretto by Blake
    Morrison, with music by Gavin Bryars,
    adapted from the novella by Jules
    Verne
Directed by Atom Egoyan
English National Opera, London, 1998

144 Sketches from the notebook: Organiz-
    ing the stage
    Photo: Courtesy of Michael Levine
145 Act 1: The dark crystalline world
    Photo: Simon Gibault
146 Act 1: Injection of gas evidence of
    electricity. Booms of lighting instru-
    ments brought in
    Photo: Simon Gibault
147 Act 2: Suffused with gas
    Photo: Simon Gibault
148 Act 2: The gas has subsided
    Photo: Simon Gibault

KEN MACDONALD

The Imaginary Invalid by Molière
Directed by Morris Panych
The Arts Club Theatre, Granville, 1996

149 Set: Into the corner
    Photo: Ken MacDonald
150 Set detail: The chair
    Photo: Ken MacDonald
151 Set detail: Confirming perspective
    Photo: Ken MacDonald

The Game of Love and Chance by Pierre
    Marivaux
Directed by Morris Panych
The Arts Club, Granville, 1996

152 Set
    Photo: Ken MacDonald
153 Set detail: Along the upstage wall
    Photo: Ken MacDonald

Waiting for the Parade by John Murrell
Directed by Glynis Leyshon
Vancouver Playhouse, 1995

154 The station house
    Photo: Ken MacDonald

7 Stories by Morris Panych
Directed by Morris Panych
Arts Club Theatre, Seymour Street, 1989

155 Set
       Photo: Ken MacDonald

Death and the Maiden by Ariel Dorfman
Directed by John Cooper
Vancouver Playhouse, 1993

156 Set
       Photo: Ken MacDonald

White Biting Dog by Judith Thompson
Directed by Morris Panych
Tarragon Theatre, 1994

157 Set
       Photo: Ken MacDonald
158 Set detail: Wall
       Photo: Ken MacDonald
159 Set detail: Staircase
       Photo: Ken MacDonald

The Overcoat conceived and directed by
       Morris Panych and Wendy Gorling,
       based on the novella by Nicholai
       Gogol, with music by Dimitri
       Shostakovich
Vancouver Playhouse, 1997

160 The set
       Photo: Ken MacDonald
161 Set detail: The pens
       Photo: Ken MacDonald
162 Architect's office with drafting table
       Photo: Ken MacDonald
163 Bedroom/Asylum
       Photo: Ken MacDonald

2000 by Joan McLeod
Directed by Morris Panych
Tarragon Theatre, 1996

164 Set: Terrarium and kitchen
       Photo: Ken MacDonald
165 Through the terrarium
       Photo: Ken MacDonald
166 Upstage to Grandmother's bedroom
       Photo: Ken MacDonald
167 Set detail: Kitchen
       Photo: Ken MacDonald

2000 by Joan McLeod
Directed by Patrick MacDonald
Vancouver Playhouse, 1997

168 Overlapping set details
       Photo: Ken MacDonald
169 The forest
       Photo: Ken MacDonald
170 View of the dining room and kitchen
       Photo: Ken MacDonald

Anatol by Arthur Schnitzler
Director by Glynis Leyshon
Belfry Theatre, 1992

171 Set with slide projection
       Photo: Ken MacDonald

Hamlet by William Shakespeare
Directed by Morris Panych
The Arts Club, Stanley Theatre, 1998

172 Set with blue upstage wall
       Photo: Ken MacDonald
173 Set with red upstage wall
       Photo: Ken MacDonald
174 Set detail: White arras
       Photo: Ken MacDonald
175 Set detail: Proscenium framing
       Photo: Ken MacDonald

The Necessary Steps by Morris Panych
Directed by Morris Panych
Arts Club Theatre, Seymour Street, 1991

176 Set
    Photo: Ken MacDonald

TERESA PRZYBYLSKI

Whale by David Holman
Directed by Maja Ardal
Young People's Theatre, 1993

177 Under the ice: Sedna surrounded by
    the whales and seals
    Photo: Brian D. Campbell

Marcel Pursued by the Hounds by Michel
    Tremblay
Directed by John van Burek
Tarragon Theatre and Pleaides Theatre,
    1998

178 Preliminary set sketch
    Private collection Teresa Przybylski
179 Preliminary set sketch
    Private collection Teresa Przybylski

A Midsummer Night's Dream by William
    Shakespeare
Directed by Jackie Maxwell
Young People's Theatre, 1993

180 Design study: Ink drawing
    Private collection Teresa Przybylski
181 Design study: Watercolour
    Private collection Teresa Przybylski
182 Design study: Watercolour
    Private collection Teresa Przybylski
183 Design study: Watercolour
    Private collection Teresa Przybylski
184 Design study: Watercolour
    Private collection Teresa Przybylski

185 Design study: Watercolour
    Private collection Teresa Przybylski
186 Costume design study: Pencil
    drawing
    Private collection Teresa Przybylski
187 Costume sketch: Quince
    Private collection Teresa Przybylski
188 Costume sketch: Helena
    Private collection Teresa Przybylski

The Serpent Woman by Carlo Gozzi
Directed by Dean Gilmour and Michèle
    Smith
Theatre Smith Gilmour, 1991

189 Costume sketch: Morgone
    Teresa Przybylski Collection

The Comedy of Errors by William Shakespeare
Directed by Richard Rose
Tom Patterson Theatre, Stratford Festival,
    1994, 1995

190 Costume sketch: Luce
    Private collection Teresa Przybylski
191 Costume sketch: Doctor
    Teresa Przybylski Collection
192 Costume sketch: Courtesan
    Teresa Przybylski Collection
193 Costume sketch: Gaoler and Officer
    Private collection Teresa Przybylski

The Emperor of Atlantis libretto by Petr Kien,
    with music by Viktor Ullman
Directed by John Neville
Canadian Opera Company, Imperial Oil
    Theatre, Joey and Toby Tanenbaum
    Centre, 1997

194 Sketch: Act 1, Harlequin and Death
    Teresa Przybylski Collection

195 Sketch: Scene 2, Emperor
Teresa Przybylski Collection
196 Sketch: Final scene
Teresa Przybylski Collection
197 Final scene
Photo: Michael Cooper
198 Costume sketch: Death
Teresa Przybylski Collection
199 Costume sketch: Soldier Woman/
Soldier
Teresa Przybylski Collection

2nd Nature by Deanne Taylor
Directed by Deanne Taylor
Hummer Sisters and VideoCabaret,
Theatre Centre, 1990

200 Costume sketch: Gusta
Teresa Przybylski Collection
201 Costume sketch: Doc
Private collection Teresa Przybylski
202 Costume sketch: Cardia
Teresa Przybylski Collection
203 Set sketch
Private collection Teresa Przybylski

Pinocchio by Maristella Roca
Directed by Richard Greenblatt
Young People's Theatre, 1993

204 Costume sketch: Pinocchio
Teresa Przybylski Collection
205 Costume sketch: Blue Water
Teresa Przybylski Collection
206 Costume sketch: Cat
Teresa Przybylski Collection
207 Costume sketch: Owl
Private collection Teresa Przybylski

INTRODUCTION
Recognizing the Place of Scenography in Canada

Scenography uses vocabularies of design of which the spectators are more or less aware – less rather than more, if the reviews are a reliable indication, for stage design seldom gets the detailed attention given to acting, dancing, music, or text. The main intention of this book is to draw attention to the designers' vocabularies, as exemplified in some notable designs by a selection of Canadian scenographers. It is also offered as a tribute to the rather undervalued achievements not only of these artists but of stage design in Canada.

Design for the stage necessarily responds to the mise en scène indicated in stage directions, dialogue, libretto, or choreography but it is by no means confined to the realization of such conceptions nor, of course, to the 'dressing' of the stage. A designer's close reading of the work to be performed reinvents the depiction of the period, characterization of the location, as well as the images and metaphors of the written text as an interplay of physical details and stage technology. Such a comprehensive approach to stage environment has to come to terms with the actuality of performance, and the role in it of a strong visual presentation. By uniting, not fragmenting, its constituent parts (set, costume, and lighting) of the design, scenography conceives the complex visual composition of the performance and its attendant technical means.

The term scenography originates in architecture and refers to drawings that represent a building as a three-dimensional object, showing the façade as well as the side walls in perspective.[1] The subsequent elision of architectural rendering with design for the stage in the definition of scenography conceives of the stage environment operating in three dimensions, rather than merely pictorially as a two-dimensional image consisting of background and foreground. Reference to the height, depth, and width of the stage and specific attention to them as integral to the performance are part of the aesthetic created for a production. That spectators are directed to look into lit spaces, at and around objects on the stage, rather than merely seeing illuminated space points to the stage space configured as volumetric and sculpted. The scale, proportions, and spatial relationships thus created in performance establish a visual context as the distribution of images in the 'space and in the flow of time'[2] rather than as a series of static scenes. The scenography becomes not only a vehicle for the narrative but actually part of the narrative that the spectator constructs.

At the same time, the scenic composition is a highly pragmatic structuring of the space that the actors inhabit and animate. Since scenography conceives of the performance environment as a kineasthetic contribution to choreographic rhythms, it can restrict the scope of the movement by the performers. Objects on stage mark the scale and proportions and punctuate the spatial relationships with the performers. As much as the actors, singers, or dancers work with the possibilities for movement in the given physical space, the spectators interpret the visual rhythms of interlocking shapes and silhouettes as integral to their perception of the stage. The costumes contribute to the visual narrative by the colour palette, cut, and texture, as grounding and enlarging the spectator's interpretation of the performance. These visual and kinesic aspects of the design are also, of necessity, intimately related to the given architecture of the venue; a proscenium arch, for example, already partly determines what is shown to the spectators, whereas the idiosyncratic and often less structured space of a reclaimed industrial building or the architectural stage of the Stratford Festival Theatre will present quite different parameters for the definition of the performance space.

As for the use of the term, scenography, it has continued to gain currency in the international community since the mid-twentieth century, when the International Organisation of Scenographers, Theatre Architects and Technicians (OISTAT) was established (1955).[3] In Canada the term has been used less frequently, perhaps. Some, but not all, of the designers considered here use the term; I have adopted it partly in response to the emphasis that all of them put on making dynamic use of the three-dimensional performance space, and partly also to associate their designs with the work of scenographers worldwide. The use of the term scenography to discuss the work by Canadian designers is also especially apt since the buildings in which theatre has been made over the last forty years have been as varied as the works written to be performed in them, and they have often incorporated the given architecture in ingenious designs.

The tremendous creativity of Canadian designers so clearly evident on local and international stages is a product of an intense development in Canadian theatre that began in the late 1960s. A highly significant part of this development has been the transformation of architectural concepts of theatre to embrace all sorts of found spaces, especially in warehouses, factories, and churches. This transformation, frequently associated with new technologies, has been deeply implicated in a heightened awareness of scenographic art as such, its power and vitality an artistic medium.

The seven scenographers considered here have been chosen partly to exhibit the breadth and originality of Canadian design in theatre, opera, and dance, but they are presented neither as 'representative' nor as an elite, but to indicate excellence, range, and variety. All have exerted influence (not always acknowledged) over stage design and have achieved at least some recognition nationally or internationally, though in quite different ways both within theatre and beyond it. Astrid Janson characteristically draws attention to the material details of the design and has made this something of a signature to her designs for productions in small and large theatres since the early 1970s, and more recently in installations at Expo '87 and the Royal Ontario Museum. Susan Benson's understanding of the implications of the architectural stage of the Stratford Festival Theatre has had significant reverberation not only at the Stratford Festival itself but also in her scenography for the Canadian Opera Company and the National Ballet of Canada. Mary Kerr's emphasis on scale and proportion has yielded highly kinetic designs for theatre, dance, and opera and also for the opening and closing ceremonies of the Commonwealth Games in the Centennial Stadium in Victoria in 1994. The 'machines for acting' designed by Jim Plaxton create a complete performance space which blends an architectonics derived from architecture with the dynamic energy of cinematography. Among the designers who have appeared on the scene since the 1980s, Michael Levine creates scenography that challenges habits of perspective as he evokes metaphors deeply imbedded in the production. Ken MacDonald emphasizes physical relationships between person and structure, and intensity of colour to create a refreshing theatricality. Teresa Przybylski's approach to scenography comes from an architect's precision of proportion and scale to create an 'event' that is fully animated by the performers. These seven are exemplary of the scope and quality of scenography in Canada.

My approach has been to highlight a few significant productions to indicate the character and range of an individual designer's work in a spectrum of architectural venues. Sketches, drawings, maquettes – materials that usually remain in the studio –

and some photographs are included in this study as the enduring and revealing embodiments of a process. Short commentaries by the designers themselves supplement the visual materials and further demonstrate the kind of awareness and techniques by which a stage design is brought into being. An understanding of this process heightens one's appreciation of finished scenography, but that finished work, like other aspects of performance, is ephemeral, and this fact adds value (and poignancy) to the material evidences of the process by which the appearance and volumetrics of the stage were defined and redefined in the studio. But it must be added that even some of the most dynamic and successful designs of the 1960s and 1970s did not always generate sketches, maquettes, technical drawings, or even pictures of the production. The records of this early phase are sparse but its importance is clearly felt in the work that came after.

Since scenographic design in Canada has been inextricable from the development of theatrical venues and companies, any account of it must register that context. The period under review, from the late 1960s to the 1999 Prague Quadrennial, has been fairly bursting with energy. At mid-century several large-scale companies had been established, such as the Stratford Festival (1953), the Canadian Opera Company (1950), the National Ballet of Canada (1951), and the Royal Winnipeg Ballet (1940). They tended to employ more established designers, and these were often from abroad.[4] These companies initially offered informal apprenticeships with a particular designer and, later, more formal programs were established, such as those at the Stratford or Shaw Festivals in the mid-1970s. When the regional theatres were established in the 1960s they opened up opportunities for both experienced and new designers. Some of the designers active in this period were Robert Doyle, Helen Campbell Tupper, Molly Harris Campbell, Frances Dafoe, Tom Doherty, Brian Jackson, Jack King, Les Lawrence, Martha Mann, Mark Negin,[5] Wallace Russell, and Eoin Sprott.[6] From the 1970s onward, as the number of theatres increased, so did the employment possibilities for designers. Among those who worked extensively during the period under discussion are Michael Eagan, Guido Tondino, John Ferguson, Ed Kotanen, Terry Gunvordhal, Maxine Graham, Cameron Porteous, Leslie Frankish, Patrick Clark, Sue LePage, Peter Hartwell, Bill Chesney, Bill Layton, Debra Hanson, Christina Poddubiuk, Evan Ayotte, Murray Laufer, Charlotte Dean, Robert Doyle, John Pennoyer, Martha Mann, Douglas Paraschuk, Steven Katz, Ted Korol, Shawn Kerwin, and Philip Silver. The training of these designers in Canada and abroad has brought a great diversity of approaches to scenography in this country, and continues to do so as many of them have taught at the National Theatre School, the Banff Centre for the Arts, and in universities and colleges.

Stepping back for a moment, a new phase in Canadian theatre may be said to have opened in 1951, when the Massey Commission issued its report,[7] and several independent theatrical ventures were initiated. Among the recommendations of the federal commission were two that emphasized the fostering of a professional theatre: one urged the founding of a facility for 'advanced training for the playwright, the producer, the technician or the actor':[8] and another proposed federal subsidies to build a network of regional theatres across the country to accommodate Canadian and foreign touring productions, with a view to stimulating local artists.[9] The Commission was not alone in entertaining such ambitions. On the local level an independent initiative of citizens in Stratford, Ontario, sought to establish a professional summer theatre in their town. The outcome of this campaign is now the stuff of a well-known history that continues to take for one of its scenes the permanent architectural stage (later modified) designed by Tanya Moiseiwitsch for the inaugural season under a tent in 1953. At the other end of the decade, in 1959, George Luscombe, Tony Ferry, Powys Thomas, and Carlo Mazzone founded Workshop Productions in a tiny basement space at 47 Fraser Avenue in Toronto.[10] It could accommodate about 60 spectators. Like the Stratford initiative, Workshop Productions took its cue from Britain, in its case from Joan Littlewood's Theatre Workshop in England.[11] Toronto Workshop Productions (the name of the company after incorporation in 1962) distinguished itself from its contemporaries by making political statements through performance, by creating its own plays, by developing a playing style appropriate to the play, and, of course, by encouraging scenographic initiatives;[12] for, like the Massey Commission and Tyrone Guthrie at Stratford, Toronto Workshop Productions had some well-defined attitudes towards design. With a mandate to develop actors and playwrights as well as designers and technicians, George Luscombe insisted that the designer be part of the creative process and attend rehearsals.

When the Massey Commission called for fully equipped theatres across the country, it meant civic auditoria that could accommodate touring productions – buildings employing conventional, well-established, and current technologies. Throughout the 1960s professional theatres were founded across the country, many with the artistic mandate for extensive touring. On the other hand, the Stratford Festival was based in an entirely distinct experiment by Tyrone Guthrie and Tanya Moiseiwitsch. The design for the Festival stage with its permanent architectural setting and proportions was inspired by Greek amphitheatres that brought with it very specific ideas about the visual aspects of performance.[13] Equally significant, but for different reasons, were George Luscombe's efforts to dispense with the architectural barriers engendered by a proscenium arch theatre as he sought to create a more immediate style of performance. Economics and politics determined how the company adapted itself to the available space in which design would emphasize a politicized performance style.

The recommendation of the Massey Commission about theatrical venues was steadily put into practice in the mandate of the Canada Council (founded in 1957) to encourage the growth of regional theatres through subsidies. In a little over a decade most urban centres across Canada had established professional theatre companies: in Halifax in 1963 the Neptune Theatre took up residence in a 525-seat, renovated vaudeville house[14] that had been used as cinema; in Winnipeg a new professional company was formed in 1958 when the Winnipeg Little Theatre and Theatre 77 merged to found the Manitoba Theatre Centre in the 800-seat Dominion Theatre; in 1962 in Vancouver the city built the 670-seat Queen Elizabeth Playhouse; in Calgary the first professional company moved into the Betty Mitchell Theatre in 1968; in Edmonton in 1965 the Citadel opened its first theatre, a 277-seat house, in the renovated former Salvation Army Citadel; in Fredericton, Theatre New Brunswick made the Beaverbrook Auditorium its base for provincial tours from 1968 to 1972, when it started to offer regular seasons in the city; and in Ottawa, the National Arts Centre, housing four theatres, was completed by 1969.[15] By this time, the Moiseiwitsch-designed stage at Stratford had been widened and in other ways modified, and in 1963 the Festival had purchased the Avon Theatre, with its proscenium stage.[16] As part of the new initiative for varied theatre productions the Charlottetown Festival, with its mandate to produce Canadian musicals, was established in the Confederation Centre in 1965. These regional theatres presented opportunities for designers across the country.

The Stratford Festival was conceived with series of professional workshops for sets, costumes, and props, as were some of the newly constructed regional theatres, but the former vaudeville houses, cinemas, or post-industrial spaces left the designers scrambling for workshop space. The Neptune Theatre, for example, did not have any workshops and Robert Doyle, who designed costumes for its first few seasons, was offered – and declined – the Artistic Director's office for two hours a day as a costume shop. 'Not accepting it,' he adds, 'I did manage to obtain what is now part of the actors' green room, a space 14' × 16' to create the clothes for the first seasons.'[17]

As for Toronto Workshop Productions (TWP), in 1967 it moved to what was to become its permanent location at 12 Alexander Street, a former Aikenhead's hardware store.[18] TWP had also established the position of a resident designer, held first by Nancy (Jowsey) Lewis and through the mid-1970s by Astrid Janson. By the time TWP had set up in Alexander Street, other non-traditional theatre venues had been opened up by small companies in Toronto with mandates for design very similar to that of TWP. Theatre Passe Muraille, initially proposing to transcend architecture altogether in performance, sprang up in Rochdale College in 1968 but in 1975 acquired an abandoned former factory, which had been saved from demolition by virtue of its historic value. The Toronto Free Theatre (established in 1972) leased premises in the former Gas Works that had recently been purchased by the Greenspoon Brothers demolition company in the hopes of developing the historic buildings into an arts complex.[19] The Factory Theatre wrested its stage and 135-seat auditorium out of the second storey of an auto repair shop and former candle factory on Dupont Street in Toronto – a space taken over in 1975 by the Phoenix Theatre. The Global Village Theatre (1969–75) established itself in a warehouse space on 17 Nicholas Street, just off Yonge Street, in a laneway off Wellesley Street. Similarly, across the country theatre artists were taking up residence in buildings other than the regional theatres: in 1973 the newly established Belfry Theatre in Victoria took over the Spring Ridge Cultural Centre which had formerly been the Emmanuel Baptist Church; in the same year the Vancouver East Cultural Centre renovated the Grandview United Church into a 350-seat theatre.

Yet another variation occurred in the relationship between theatres and the changing definition of theatre in Canada, which also had a bearing on design. Across the country theatre complexes were being assembled, acquired, or built that would accommodate both experimentation and established theatre practice. In Montreal, the Centaur Theatre took up residence at the Old Stock Exchange Building in 1969 and five years later made the building into a theatre complex with two theatres – a smaller 225-seat open stage theatre and a 440-seat proscenium theatre. In Niagara-on-the-Lake, the Shaw Festival, which began in 1962 on the second floor of the old court house, built its 840-seat mainstage Festival Theatre in 1973, and seven years later acquired the Royal George Theatre, a former vaudeville house seating 240. In 1976 the Edmonton Citadel, after eleven years in its makeshift premises, launched a new theatre complex housing three theatres – a 685-seat proscenium arch theatre, a 250-seat studio, and a multi-purpose hall seating 240. The Manitoba Theatre Centre had moved into its new 785-seat theatre by 1970 and maintained its lively experimentation in the 232-seat

Warehouse. The Stratford Festival, in response to the work being done in theatres across the country, started to rent space in a local community centre as its third, more experimental stage in 1971.[20] In 1970 the civic-spirited St Lawrence Centre for the Performing Arts was built in Toronto, housing a 500-seat and an 830-seat theatre. Eleven years after it opened, it underwent extensive renovations.[21] In 1985 Theatre Calgary moved into the Max Bell Theatre in the new Centre for the Performing Arts to share the 750-seat theatre with Alberta Theatre Projects, and in 1987 another 60-seat venue, The Secret Space, became the home of One Yellow Rabbit Performance Company.[22] Increasingly even the smaller theatres began to develop two spaces in the same venue as they renovated their premises; the Tarragon Theatre, established in 1971, added the 100-seat Extra Space in 1983. In these theatres across the country many artistic partnerships were struck by a director and a designer but most designers were freelance.

With the establishment of the Associated Designers of Canada in 1965 the significant presence of designers as theatre artists had to be acknowledged nationally. In 1967 this organization sent a delegation to the first Prague Quadrennial, an international showcase of theatre design,[23] and has done so ever since. The exhibit sent in 1979 was particularly resonant. The work of five designers was sent to Prague: Robert Prévost,[24] Michael Eagan,[25] Susan Benson,[26] Cameron Porteous,[27] and Astrid Janson.[28] Tom Doherty, president of ADC, observed that 'just as Canadian theatre companies have discovered varied styles of production dependent on the physical conditions of their buildings, so too Canadian designers have developed a wide variety of individual styles and approaches to design solutions, motivated only by the desire to excel.'[29] Astrid Janson confirmed Doherty's remark:

> For me, designing for the theatre presents a dual challenge: First of all, it provides the opportunity to break new ground by working with original scripts in a milieu that is an alternative to classical productions, large budgets and conventional theatre architecture ... When working with converted spaces renovated warehouses, churches, factories where seating is seldom more than 350, I try to meet the challenges that these limitations present by originating a design which embraces the entire space, including the audience ... to attempt to bind the aesthetics to the action on stage; to discover an integral stage form which captures the heartbeat of the work.[30]

Susan Benson, who had designed primarily in proscenium arch theatres before coming to Stratford, articulated the challenge launched by Tanya Moiseiwitsch for design on the Stratford Festival Stage, where the architecture calls for a 'simpler approach' and where design 'tends to be focused on the costumes which I think should be an extension of the actor's character rather than just adornment.'[31]

When the Associated Designers of Canada mounted the exhibition 'Stage Design in Canada, 1994–1998: A Prelude to Prague,' they featured the work of twenty-four designers from across Canada.[32] From this exhibit a jury selected the work of Susan Benson, Raymond Marcus-Boucher, Robert Gardiner, Michael Levine, Ken MacDonald, Christina Poddubiuk, Cameron Porteous, Teresa Przybylski, Philip Silver, and Allan Stitchbury to represent Canada at the 1999 Prague Quadrennial. Philip Silver, in his remarks in the exhibition brochure, observed that 'the growth and achievement of stage design across Canada has paralleled that of the Stratford Festival. In the years following the Festival's 1953 founding and particularly in the late 1960s, a remarkable burst of activity occurred – the founding of the Shaw Festival, the establishment of major "regional" theatres in many large Canadian cities and the experimentation of new playwrights and directors. One of the happy results was the increased opportunities for designers to practice their art.'[33] In this exhibit Teresa Przybylski's design for the Tarragon was one of the very few examples from a small theatre. A reason for this is that designs for larger theatres tend to produce more elaborate and inviting evidences of their process. In this study I have also felt that temptation to concentrate on larger productions but I have tried to convey the distinction and interest of work on a small scale, as well as that of grander manifestations.

Aptly enough, Philip Silver added the cautionary note that while designers were regularly part of local award ceremonies[34] the critical discussion of their work was much less evident. This was true enough but the remark itself was an indication that such discussion was underway. Canadian theatre magazines and journals *Scene Changes, Performing Arts in Canada, Theatrum, Canadian Theatre Review*, and *Theatre Research in Canada* offered profiles of specific designers or productions during the 1970s and 1980s. In the 1990s *Canadian Theatre Review* devoted two issues to scenography,[35] and often refers to particular designs. There have been exhibitions of the work of designers at the Stratford[36] and Shaw Festivals[37] but scenography remains obscure in the histories of such theatre companies as the Royal Winnipeg Ballet,[38] Théâtre du Rideau Vert,[39] and Théâtre du Nouveau Monde[40] in Montreal. Remarkable in this context are the two catalogues produced by Association des Professionnels des Arts de la Scène du Québec, which bring into view the diversity of design in Quebec from 1940 to 1994,[41] and the record of productions of Théâtre Ubu in Montreal between 1982 and 1994.[42] *L'Annuaire théâtral* also devoted a special issue to the study of scenography, and two special issues of *Les Cahiers du théâtre, Jeu* have featured interviews, artists' statements, and theoretical articles exploring methods of analysis.[43] These publications devoted specifically to scenography in Quebec, with its distinct development of spaces and dramaturgy, are worthy of emulation elsewhere in the country.

If this volume encourages further discussion of scenography in Canada it will have achieved one of its most important objectives. It is intended also as a contribution to both the history and the appreciation of design and thus as an enhancement of the pleasure of theatre-going. It attempts to mark moments when the scenography for a production has been envisioned most intensely. The sketches, maquettes, and photos are presented as insights into a process, not, of course, a reconstitution of the effects achieved in production. All the designers have been generous in the descriptions of their work and the reader is encouraged to read them as a sequence as well as individually since their effect is partly cumulative. My own commentary and analysis, accompanying the quotations and the photos, is informed not only by archival records and interviews but also, in many cases, by attendance at the production referred to, and has involved thinking back from a final theatrical impression. Ultimately the volume attempts the impossible task of trying to convey on the page ideas about a moving spectacle.

1

ASTRID JANSON

Astrid Janson started her professional career after completing a degree in philosophy at the University of Waterloo and an MA in design at the University of British Columbia. Her first professional association was with the Toronto Dance Theatre, where she was a costume designer for the 1972–3 season.[1] Her dynamic approach was a very good match for the company's choreography, inspired as it was by the athleticism and angularity of Martha Graham. (Her costumes for *Baroque Suite* and *Boat, River, Moon* were still in evidence at the company's twenty-fifth anniversary performances twenty years later.) In the fall of 1973 Janson began her long association with George Luscombe at Toronto Workshop Productions. There, she held the position of resident designer until 1977, after which she continued her association with the company for another five years as a freelance designer.[2] Between 1975 and 1984[3] she worked as a designer at the Canadian Broadcasting Corporation,[4] continued as a freelancer, and made her first designs for the Shaw[5] and Stratford[6] Festivals. At Stratford, her command of the 40-foot thrust stage of the Tom Patterson Theatre[7] has been particularly significant in designs for emotionally charged readings of plays in which Martha Henry has acted. Janson's association with this actor-director dates back to collaborations in Toronto in the 1980s,[8] and continued during Henry's tenure as Artistic Director of the Grand Theatre in London from 1988 to 1995 (when Janson designed more than ten productions) and their collaboration at the Citadel in Edmonton.[9]

In the 1970s, Janson designed for small companies such as Theatre Compact,[10] Global Village Theatre,[11] and the Tarragon Theatre;[12] by the 1980s she was designing for larger venues: Young People's Theatre,[13] the National Ballet of Canada,[14] Royal Winnipeg Ballet,[15] Toronto Arts Productions[16] and Centre Stage[17] in the St Lawrence Centre, Toronto Free Theatre, the Canadian Opera Company, and the Desrosiers Dance Company.[18] She also designed for smaller companies such as Nightwood Theatre[19] and VideoCabaret[20] when they emerged in the 1980s. In the United States she has designed for the Opera Company of Philadelphia[21] and the University of Michigan School of Music.[22] During the 1990s she designed at Canadian Stage, the Citadel, the National Arts Centre, the Stratford Festival, the Factory Theatre, and the Tarragon, as well as for smaller companies that do musicals, such as Eclectic Theatre. Her work has been recognized by seven Dora Mavor Moore Awards for costume and set design, and a Toronto Drama Bench Award for Distinguished Contribution to Canadian Theatre in 1980. She first represented Canada at the Prague Quadrennial in 1979, and in 1998 she served on the jury to select the Canadian delegation. In 1998 she was appointed as a part-time instructor in the Drama Program at University College at the University of Toronto.

Janson has designed not only for theatre, television, opera, dance, and film, but for exhibitions also. In 1978 she designed 400 costumes for Conklin and Garrett's *All Canadian Antique Carnival* at the Calgary Stampede; in 1986 she created eleven sets depicting the history of the province for the Ontario Pavilion at Expo in Vancouver; and during the summer of 1998, she returned to installation work with a design for the hands-on Discovery Gallery at the Royal Ontario Museum. These commissions, especially the latter two, demonstrate a recognition of Janson's ability to animate space, not only by what is presented but also by the attention to scale and proportion, as in her theatre scenography.

Astrid Janson's approach to scenography might be characterized as always drawing the spectators into the performance rather than simply contextualizing the performers. To this end, she tends to elaborate crucial elements or details and to exploit fully their interaction with light. Her choice of details is always made with an acute awareness of the size of the theatre and the proximity of the spectators to enjoy the details. For the production of *Charming and Rose*[23] at the 100-seat Theatre Centre, for example, the ironic monument to princessdom was the pink ball gown, constructed out of foam rubber, which became a soft sculpture when it was not being worn, and accreted meaning as a figuration of public splendour coupled with private abuse. Janson emphasized Rose's isolation by giving the impression of this tiny chamber as her prison in the tower, and reinforced this image by making access, and thus departure, arduous – through an opening high up on the wall reachable only by climbing a ladder.

One of Janson's favourite techniques is the use of projections onto such varied materials as plexiglass, balloons, elastic fabric, fabric, garbage bags, and scrim, to make them transparent or opaque and animate the stage. Janson described the flexibility in her design for *Passion*[24] where she used a multi-panelled screen made out of wire mesh in combination with technologically enhanced slides: 'When the large screen was lit from various angles it could seem to be the stone walls of the fortress, or lit differently, its transparency could present the interior walls of several rooms into which the audience could see, or when lit with projections could be transformed instantaneously into the garden walls. The collaged images served to change locales by a change in lighting with minor changes to the set.' Actors could be silhouetted against this wall, which could also be made transparent by Paul Mathiesen's lighting design so as to expand the stage space instantaneously and effortlessly.

The use of everyday objects on stage as contributions to a visual narrative is another Janson strategy. The spectators recognize the constituent elements of the set as they read it. A production of *The Master Builder*,[25] for example, used plastic packaging for the panes of glass in the highly stylized French doors, which drew the spectators' attention to the material constituents of the stage world as intrusions from a different present reality. Here, as elsewhere, her scenography probed the metaphorical structure of the production and created a kinetic environment that enabled frequent changes of perspective.

You Can't Get Here from There by Jack Winter (Toronto Workshop Productions, 1974–5)

> The task was to transform the location without moving scenery. The set had to change from an embassy to exterior locations through lighting or by varying the use of material. The solution was a plexiglass cube, the walls of which all pivoted so that they could virtually disappear when set at angles to the audience. The upstage wall was stationary, covered in white carpet and used as a projection screen. The Embassy was pure white in contrast to the colour slides projected onto the cube. We used film images of 'The Disappeared' and marching troops as well as slides of colour, such as red spatters of blood which were detectable on the reflective front walls, but were unmistakably projected on the white embassy wall as well as on the actors. (ASTRID JANSON)

A crucial element of Janson's scenography is finding the appropriate materials and textures for the way in which she would like the physical elements to interact with light. For the set of *You Can't Get Here from There*, Jack Winter's theatrical critique of the Canadian government's response to the coup in Chile, Janson assembled a large cube that dominated the stage.[26] Two walls of this cube were transparent and could pivot to allow entry while the other two were stationary, opaque, and, like the floor, covered in white carpet. The scenography was a strongly signifying contribution to the work. It was a 'huge display case or store window into which the Chilean refugees could peer, but only rarely penetrate.'[27] Janson made further use of the front panels of the cube as a screen on which documentary images of the Chilean disaster were projected: tanks in the streets and dissidents rounded up in a soccer stadium. The juxtaposition of the immediate theatrical event with the documentary images created a powerful visual dynamic between the actors and the narratizing slides. Janson's projections onto the walls of the cube were a conscious rejection of stage painting. The trompe l'oeil effect of the transparent walls both opened up the stage space completely and at the same time severely constrained the choreography.

In later productions Janson experimented with the interplay of light and materials. For Theatre Compact's production of Hugh Leonard's *Da* (1976) she projected images onto a backdrop of giant balloons. For Beverly and Raymond Pannell's *Refugees* (1979), a cooperative production by Toronto Workshop Productions and Co-Opera Theatre, she created a highly dynamic environment. For this story of two Jewish families emigrating from Europe to Canada between 1930 and 1975, she contrived an unspecific and inhospitable 'temporary waiting space' out of 1,200 plastic milk crates, anticipating a lighting design that would cast shadows through the grids of the base and sides of the crates when lamps were placed inside them. But perhaps her most dynamic use of slides was in the production *The Mac Paps* (1980), by George Luscombe and Larry Cox. For this play about the Mackenzie-Papineau Battalion in the Spanish Civil War, Janson devised a stunning and disturbing sequence in which blood-spattered images of war alternated with slides of Picasso's *Guernica*. The 'screen' in this case was a wall made of elastic strips stretched taut. When the actors passed through the wall they distorted the images.

Les Canadiens by Rick Salutin with an assist by Ken Dryden (Centaur Theatre, 1977; Toronto Workshop Productions, 1977)

The problem was to create a feeling of being in an arena full of fans and their fanaticism. At the Centaur Theatre, which has a proscenium arch, my solution was to use sliding panels of fabric to create a moiré effect, a dizzying effect, as the painted circles suggesting packed stands of fans were animated. In Toronto, at Toronto Workshop Productions I could create an arena audience, by placing life-size soft sculptures of fans, surrounding the stage on three sides. These fans were placed so that they were also useful as a barrier or embankment for the actors who would come down the ramps on skateboards and rollerskates. One of the actors talked to several fans placed in the audience, became angry and engaged in a fight with one. (ASTRID JANSON)

Janson's scenography for the first two productions of *Les Canadiens* realized the playwright's metaphorical and literal representation of ice hockey as the premise for an exploration of historical and cultural tensions between French and English Canadians, figured as the Toronto Maple Leafs and the Montreal Canadiens. For the production in Montreal at the Centaur Theatre in the spring of 1977, Janson re-envisioned the stage as the Montreal Forum, home of the Canadiens. Her design cast the spectators as fans and used a backdrop of abstract images representing tiers of imagined spectators facing the real ones. This other crowd was created using two layers of cloth on which Janson painted concentric circles to suggest faces and which during crucial moments in the action was made to appear animated by light striking the backdrop as the layers of fabric were slid in opposite directions.

In Toronto Janson continued with her experimentation and on this occasion transformed the large black box auditorium into a miniature version of the Montreal Forum. Brechtian signs announcing the scenes were flashed on the notice-cum scoreboard, and the actors dressed in costumes modelled on the uniforms of the rival teams, glided on roller skates down ramps encircling the rink, stage or simulated skating in their running shoes. To complete the sense of the arena Janson introduced a mezzanine level and placed on it human-size mannequins (among them a playful likeness of the playwright himself) but dressed in costumes of the nineteenth century.[28] In Toronto, of course, the production had a further resonance of 'Hockey Night in Canada,'[29] since Maple Leaf Gardens, then the home of the Maple Leafs, was only about a block away from TWP's former theatre.

History of the Village of the Small Huts and *The Global Village* by Michael Hollingsworth (VideoCabaret at the Theatre Centre and Factory Theatre Café, 1992–7)

Every costume must work on a number of levels. Big and shiny is not enough: the next layer emerges as it is related to the character. The political layer is achieved in the tableaux.

The costumes for these productions with very quick changes need to be practical, visually fun, represent the character with wit, signal political clarification to the audience, and be inexpensive and be durable. (ASTRID JANSON)

Janson's most striking costumes are those for the ten productions she had designed for VideoCabaret by 1998. Her association with VideoCabaret began with costumes for *Tory, Tory, Tory* (1985), and she designed costumes for the last three installments of *History of the Village of the Small Huts* (1992–4)[30] and the three plays of *The Global Village* (1994–7).[31] The rootedness of the company in performance art has engendered a cartoon-like style of performance for its satirical presentation of Canadian history and politics. Its shows are structured as a succession of quick scenes, staged in a black box created specifically for *History of the Village of the Small Huts* and *The Global Village*[32] or in a high-tech mock-up of television studios.[33] For VideoCabaret Janson often installs the actors in inflated, larger-than-life costumes, which make incisive commentaries in themselves – as they must, for the actors are seen against a purely black background for only a couple of minutes. Most of these shows involve more than one hundred rapid costume changes and each costume and prop must convey an immediate social and political context. These costumes are witty combinations of surprising fabrics and magnified props, often harking back to identifiable 'portraits' that have now become part of the country's mythology. The costumes mimic period clothes but in a style of high parody. In small spaces seating about 150 spectators, moreover, the proximity of the spectators is a crucial factor in the design of details. For *The Great War* the olive green jackets of the military uniforms were made from a shiny laminate fabric and were sewn to pad out the actor, and the military medals turned out, on close inspection, to be bottle caps and plastic fruits. In *The Life and Times of Mackenzie King* the checkered suit of the séance-haunting Prime Minister was created from a silver and black lamé fabric altogether appropriate for a theatrical revenant of a spiritualist persuasion. In the installments of *The Global Village* Janson's costumes limned out portraits of the human interest stories both of the postwar nuclear family, with all its accoutrements for better suburban living, and the irreverent but eerily accurate icons of politicians, such as Pierre Elliott Trudeau in his buckskin jacket.

For the multimedia cabarets, held to coincide with contemporary political events – the federal election in 1993, the Quebec Referendum in 1995, and the recent instalment of the work-in-progress *Vox Pop Cabarets – The VideoCabaret News* in 1998 – Janson's parodies of newsdesk chic was unabashed. And her carnivalesque use of maple leaf fabric for the costumes in 1998 was strong medicine for Canadian political fever and the sick-room atmosphere that attends it.

Molly Sweeney by Brian Friel (Canadian Stage Company, Bluma Appel Theatre, 1998)

> I tried to create a strong but imperceptible change in the set during the performance – to see what the audience would notice and whether they would engage with what is happening internally on the stage. As Molly's world became more internal the set curled around the characters and created an entirely different world. Even though the play is a tragedy there is a visual comfort on the stage as the central character makes a conscious choice about her life and death. (ASTRID JANSON)

Woman in Mind by Alan Ayckbourn (Grand Theatre, 1991)

> The set started from a green hole that by the end of the show was covered with 24-foot-high wild growth, including tendrils of slinkies falling out of the sky. The whole world changes and no one notices; the idea that our own real life is dull in comparison to our fantasies is a very strong 20th century message. As the woman becomes more enmeshed in her fantasy family the garden grows up around them during the performance in view of the audience. The fantasy family begins to scale the walls of a metal cage in the centre of the stage, that the woman's real family cannot even see. (ASTRID JANSON)

For *Molly Sweeney* Janson substantially changed the perception of the large proscenium theatre by animating the floor rather than the walls or the upstage area. With a gently raked zigzagging ramp to draw the eye upstage, Janson distinguished this floor as a reflective white surface. In the vertical axis she used eight columns made of scrim that could be lit by Robert Thomson's lighting with patterned projections as though catching the light from the sun and later appear luminous in the moonlight. Initially the columns dominated the stage and carried connotations of the monumentality of tragedy. But the emphasis on the columns faded as the ramps imperceptibly disengaged from the wings and curled towards the centre stage. When the chairs on the ramp did not tip over, but followed the line of the floor, it became evident that the set change was also a shift in its *raison d'être*. It was no longer indicating an objective reality but redefining the spatial organization to create a fresh structure. In essence Janson transformed the ramp to make the stage a containing structure that resembled the ribs and stem of a boat. This destabilization of the spectator's perception of the visual prepared the way for the ethical questions posed by Friel.

With this scenography Janson brought her own emphasis on three dimensionality into a proscenium arch theatre. As the design evolved in performance spectators could not help but imagine the set from the upstage looking towards the auditorium and consider how the actors accommodated themselves to this gradually changing floor. In effect the stage became a silent character in the production that brought home the significance of visual as well as verbal dialogue for the audience.

Janson had redirected the spectator's understanding of the stage with a similar design in the Grand Theatre for *Woman in Mind*, when, during the intermission, a wild garden started to grow into an upstage wall of vegetation. The vividly coloured plants were sewn onto a mesh that was drawn up slowly into the flies, from which coloured plastic slinkie toys dropped as tendrils. Eventually the spectator was more visually engrossed in the representation of the woman's imagination, since the garden 'grew' in sync with her dissociation from her family, than in the apparently simpler reality of the human relationships. These two designs demonstrate how Janson has been able to effectively bring the significance of free-standing scenery into the sightlines of a proscenium arch theatre and encourages the spectator to take in two narratives simultaneously.

The Cherry Orchard by Anton Chekhov (Festival Theatre, Shaw Festival, 1981; Tom Patterson Theatre, Stratford Festival, 1998)

In both, the major design problem was the location of the orchard. I solved it at the Shaw Festival by making it a constant presence, but the physical space of the Tom Patterson invited a different solution.

At the Shaw, when the orchard is chopped down the lace hangings came to rest on the stage and the cyclorama is torn down with horrible sounds of it ripping to reveal the walls of the actual theatre. By this destruction of the cherry orchard my intent was to show the move from the 19th-century theatrical world to the modern technology of the 20th century. With all the lace down the audience could see the equipment of the theatre just as the illusions on the stage were being stripped away.

At the Stratford Festival, the design was dictated by the shape and sightlines of the

Tom Patterson Theatre. The idea was that the different rooms could be easily changed; that the actors could manipulate the curtains to change them. The difference in budget between the two productions meant that we could not consider the Stratford production as the same kind of major undertaking that the Shaw Festival one was. It was very difficult to place the orchard on the stage in a way that did not seem totally artificial when the characters spoke. Hanging a swing downstage helped pull the audience towards the orchard in the fourth wall. A great bonus at the Tom Patterson Theatre is the intimacy of the audience. (ASTRID JANSON)

The scenography for the two productions of *The Cherry Orchard* demonstrates how Janson integrates light and textures rather than furniture upon the stage. In 1981 at the Shaw Festival Janson took advantage of the fly tower of the Festival Theatre and created a design that balanced suspended elements with those that were wheeled in. The design emphasized the height of the stage using the lace hangings that overlapped, to fill up the volume, presenting the spectators with the orchard in bloom, but did so by highlighting a carefully wrought world that was also very fragile. The ancillary stages that Janson devised were inserted into the orchard setting: for the outdoor scene of Act 2 a large white 'quilt,' a third of the width of the stage, descended from the flies, and remained partially suspended from its bar as a backdrop shielding the characters from the orchard, while the rest of it served as the blanket on the ground. By contrast, for the interior scenes, chandeliers descended among the lace hangings and rooms were created on a small platform, similar in size to the 'quilt' but with a slight rake, on which the furniture defined the location. When the lace and cyclorama were torn down in the final sequence and the starkness of the backstage wall was exposed, the bourgeois longing for theatrical illusion was fully registered and a powerful effect achieved by denying this satisfaction. The costumes that Janson designed for this production continued the nuances of the antique lace hangings, repeating similar details: the fabrics she chose were tricot or loose weaves, and all the costumes were in cream or light pastel shades, highly stylized, evoking fragility and fluidity.[34]

At the Tom Patterson Theatre, seventeen years later, Janson created a visual rhythm that provided a very different sense of the orchard. As in all the productions she has designed in this theatre, Janson used the imposing upstage area to create a dominant image, rather than to represent a location. She used the monumentally proportioned architecture of the upstage wall as a projection screen for the orchard.[35] That it was twice as high as any real cherry tree made it proportionally more immediately present for the spectator as an evanescent image of time in the production. Employing the height and length of the 40-foot thrust stage she balanced the presentation of indoor and outdoor environments by drawing attention to parts of the stage in a distinct manner. The outdoor scenes emphasized the full height of the theatre; the cherry orchard was integrated into the very fabric of the stage as before, but in this theatre, she used projections of trees on the curtains on the upstage wall. Janson balanced this imposing presence of the trees with a swing at the other end of the thrust stage, linking the two extremes by petals scattered between them. For the interior scenes Janson created a more intimate stage, defining the rooms with carpets and a few chairs, and with the apostrophized bookcase located upstage. And when the upstage curtains were opened they gave forth onto the ballroom, very far from the audience. The effect of this scenography was to insinuate the spectators into the scenes by dividing up the space in two axes so as to change their spatial perceptions.

Reflections EXPO '86 Vancouver

> The central challenge was to represent the history of Ontario without words, illustrating events and time periods by different theatrical settings. The pavilion was designed as a walk through history and the audience followed a spiral path through the building. To get the audience into a quieter mood, slides of paintings by the Group of Seven, Tom Thomson, Lawren Harris, and some historical paintings of *coureurs de bois* were projected onto screens made of scrim. The exhibit of the English and French battle for supremacy on the Plains of Abraham in 1759 played with extreme scale, where each of the figures was about 16 feet high and the spectators walked between them. The two kings, Louis XV and George II, had Montcalm and Wolfe impaled on their thumbs, while their ship mobiles represented their fleets sailing slowly in the air currents. To show Confederation, I created a miniature theatre with Sir John A. Macdonald balancing on both a French and a British horse. He was being applauded by famous Ontarians, each of whom was represented as a tin toy about 8" high. For the modern period, images of contemporary stars of Ontario culture were projected onto clear acrylic tubes. The picture would come in and out of focus as the tubes pivoted growing longer and shorter. (ASTRID JANSON)

Janson's two large installation projects characteristically inform the viewers by animating the objects. The eleven exhibits of *Reflections* provided a tour of the history industry, and natural splendour of the province of Ontario. Janson very carefully calculated the scale in relation to the spectator, so that spectators experienced the simulated thunder of Niagara Falls and the overwhelming colour 'sculpture' of the slag heap created by the nickel smelters in Sudbury. She represented historical moments in two exhibits that varied greatly in scale and, characteristically for Janson, politicized Canada's own efforts at self-mythologization. The presentation of battles for the colony in the eighteenth century had the spectators walk between the two giants, only to encounter the figure of Uncle Sam, presaging the American bid for the territory in the War of 1812. Further along Janson depicted Ontario's role in Confederation as a circus routine in a miniaturized theatre. This exhibit also defied a simple enactment of the story of a nation. She integrated the sections of the walk by the use of light: slides of paintings would fade as the next one lit up to draw the spectator onwards. In the exhibit's final section Janson focussed on contemporary culture, using projections on plastic tubes set at various angles to their platforms and rotated from below by small motors so as to alter the projected images.

In 1998, Janson designed the Discovery Gallery, a hands-on exhibit for children at the Royal Ontario Museum. The gallery comprises eight distinct themes and at its centre stands the full-scale replica of a Tyrannosaurus Rex. Visitors are free to move through the gallery at their own pace, and are encouraged to investigate the exhibits in various ways. They can view the dinosaur from a boardwalk that traces the neck and curve of the spine before descending along the tail, or they can engage in the archaeological recovery of footprints in the sand at the base of the model. Janson differentiated the sections primarily by colour on the walls, and created environments for each area where the visitors can develop an approach to the topic: in the Lab, activity boxes are stored in a cabinet and the children are encouraged to take a box to a nearby table, while in the Collector's Corner, some of the items are behind glass, while others are facsimiles of artefacts available to touch, and still others offer themselves for identification. In the Workshop a large painted buffalo skin under glass, several ancient Chinese painted tiles, and an ancient vase behind glass form the parameters of an activity centre where paper, crayons and pencils are available to transform impressions into pictures and stories. Throughout, the design is conceived as a means of animating the young visitors, pleasing and informing them.

COSTUME SKETCHES

The Glass Menagerie by Tennessee Williams (Tarragon Theatre, 1998)

> This drawing illustrates how I think of costume drawings in relation to the play. I often choose a moment when something significant is happening to the character. The costume is then essential to appreciating the presence of the character. In this sketch the moment between Amanda and Laura captures the intimacy between mother and daughter. Just outside the beam of the spotlight are the details of the costume, the shoes for Amanda and the front view of her dress and a stronger wash of the colour for her costume. (ASTRID JANSON)

Astrid Janson's sketches for costumes insist on their own impressions of the realization of the character in performance. In the sketches for Amanda and Laura's costumes in *The Glass Menagerie* Janson isolates the two figures in a shaft of light. The sketch deliberately separates the cut of the dresses, shown in the pencil drawing, from their colour. She includes the colour for the dresses as the delicate wash of the turquoise in the upper right-hand corner, equivalent to a fabric swatch. She gives a further impression of the colour for the costume by creating a delicate border in the turquoise shades that are clearly present in the chiffon fabric called for. The design for the set brought in the sense of lightness as it contrasted scrim walls with the brise-block walls of the theatre itself.

Long Day's Journey into Night by Eugene O'Neill (Tom Patterson Theatre, 1994, 1995, 1998)

> The sketch for Mary Tyrone in Act 2 surrounds her with the colours of her house, but also the fog that leaves her isolated in a gentler, softer space all her own. The details of the wedding dress that she brings downstairs are repeated in this scene as she is dressed in lace at the neck drifting into the easy folds of the bodice and sleeves, and the gently flared cuffs gathered to the arm with pearl buttons. (ASTRID JANSON)

Rusalka by Anton Dvořák (Opera Company of Philadelphia, 1988) and **Incognito** by Robert Desrosiers (Calgary Olympics, 1988)

Costumes which transform the human figure have many possibilities in dance. The dancers were also an extension of the set, manipulating the layers of silk fabrics representing the sea. (ASTRID JANSON)

In the sketches for Mary Tyrone in *Long Day's Journey into Night* Janson uses a pencil drawing for the figure so that the significant details of the costume – the neckline and the details of the sleeves – can be introduced into the characterization of the role to which the garment might contribute. In the case of sketch 'Mary Tyrone 2' Janson adds an extra feature, an outline of the whole figure, rather than using shading to present the figure's three-dimensionality. Using swirls of watercolour, where the blue, black, and sand have been allowed to bleed into each other, Janson does not allow the colour to intrude upon the figure and in this way she provides both a sense of the features of the garment but as well its presence on stage.

The costumes for *Rusalka* and *Incognito* have been grouped together, even though one is for opera and the other for dance, because they provide excellent examples of the emphasis that Janson places on altering the body in performance. The theme for Robert Desrosiers's dance was 'human disguise' in a ballet that deals with layers of being and potentiality. Janson's costumes allowed the spectator to see how the body of the dancer had been transformed into this figure, to become a creature of a different order. On the stage the rhythm and movement of a dancer's body become fully evident, not merely as technique but as narrative expression. In these sketches one sees how costumes can make their contribution to the story.

SUSAN BENSON

Susan Benson completed her studies at the West of England College of Art / Bristol University in 1963. She went on to work as a designer at the BBC and the Royal Shakespeare Company before emigrating to Canada in 1966. As a freelance designer Benson worked in British Columbia at the Vancouver Playhouse, Holiday Theatre, Children's Centennial Theatre, and Simon Fraser University, and in Ontario at the University of Windsor. In 1970 she was appointed as assistant professor and resident designer at the Krannert Center for the Performing Arts at the University of Illinois.[1] During her four years there she designed half a dozen operas, four dance presentations, and over thirty plays and musicals. In 1974 Benson began her association with the Stratford Festival as a designer at the Third Stage, then in its third season.[2] In the following year she added the other two Stratford stages to her credits, designing *Twelfth Night* for the Festival Stage and Arthur Miller's *The Crucible* for the Avon. In 1981 she became the head of design at Stratford – a position she held until 1983 – and in 1995 she was appointed an associate director of the Stratford Festival. Besides her work at Stratford, she has designed productions in theatres across Canada, among them the National Arts Centre, the Vancouver Playhouse, Manitoba Theatre Centre, Theatre New Brunswick, London's Grand Theater, Neptune Theatre, Citadel Theatre, and Young People's Theatre. In the United States she has designed for the Guthrie Theatre in Minneapolis[3] and the Denver Center Theater Company. She has also designed for the Royal Winnipeg Ballet,[4] and the National Ballet of Canada.[5] She has designed opera for the Banff Centre for the Arts,[6] the Guelph Spring Festival,[7] and for many companies, including the Canadian,[8] New York City,[9] Minnesota,[10] Seattle, Australian,[11] and St Louis Opera Companies. Benson's scenography was represented at five of the six Prague Quadrennial exhibitions between 1979 and 1999. Besides teaching at the University of Illinois, Susan Benson has taught at the National Theatre School in Montreal, York University, the Banff School of Fine Arts, the University of Victoria, the University of Michigan, the University of Alberta, and Master classes for the United States Institute of Theatre Technology. She continues teaching while working as a freelance designer.

Susan Benson is a painter as well as a scenographer, and the dynamic tension between the two disciplines is felt in her distinctive design vocabulary. Her work has been the focus of several exhibitions. At Gallery Stratford her set and costume designs were exhibited in *Design Made Glorious* (1977)[12] and *A Most Rare Fashion* (1981), while her theatre portraits were the subject of a solo exhibit at Gallery 96 in Stratford in 1984. Also in 1984, her work was included in two group shows in Toronto, *Stage Rite* at Harbourfront, and *Designing Ladies* at the Ontario Craft Council Gallery (paintings and designs). In 1986 her designs were part of the Stratford Festival's exhibit *It Was a Lover and His Lass* in the main gallery of the Lincoln Center's Library and Museum of Performing Arts. In 1989 Gallery Stratford mounted the solo exhibit *Susan Benson Artist / Designer*. Her work has earned many awards: a Guthrie, an Ace, a Jessie Richardson, a Sterling, and no fewer than six Dora Mavor Moore Awards. In 1986 she was elected to the Royal Canadian Academy of Arts and in 1993 she received a Canada Council Senior Arts Award for independent artistic research and study in Italy.[13]

As painter and designer, Benson is two different kinds of artist. The painter has to assume total control over the composition but the scenographer keeps firmly in mind the creative roles of director and actors and the demands of the audience. Working for the director, Benson's primary concern is to define the three-dimensionality of the production; for the actor, she likes to realize small, often personal, details in the costume that will help with the evocation of another time; for the spectator, she searches for details that will signify a historical period and its distinctiveness. She sketches the costumes before she designs the sets, approaching scenography through colour and texture. Benson's costume sketches for *A Midsummer Night's Dream* (1976 and 1977) indicate how the concept of the costume leads into an overall style for the production. There is also a painterly aspect to some of her designs: for *The Marriage of Figaro* (1990) she referred to neoclassical landscape paintings in the murals used to convey a visual narrative instead of interior sets.

Benson's costume drawings use a painter's media – pastels, watercolours, or oils – to approach production design. The pastel crayons for *Madama Butterfly*, the dripped-oil sketches for *The Woman*, and the solid blocks of colour and watercolour splatters for

Cabaret each evince a distinctive texture for the production. Without necessarily including a background for the figure, a Benson costume sketch constitutes a gloss on her conception of the character through the posture and gesture of the figure, while the fabric and cut of the costume convey a sense of the space that a character will take up (both on stage and in the spectator's imagination). Juxtaposing, for example, the sketches for *Cabaret, Madama Butterfly,* and *The Woman*, one sees quite different ideas of a stage presence: the figures for *Cabaret* are near-photographic, at rest or posing, but the pastel drawings for *Madama Butterfly* suggest the movement of the character in a costume that is meant to be viewed not just from the front but from the side and in motion. Differently again, the drawings for *The Woman* present the statuesque, resolved, figure in front of a massive background which holds her in a tight focus. In each case, the visual impact that Benson wishes the character to achieve in performance establishes a vocabulary for the scenographic conception overall.

A Midsummer Night's Dream by William Shakespeare (Stratford Festival, Festival Stage, 1976, 1977)

Robin Phillips had a very strong visual concept for the production. Basically it was the positive and negative worlds of the court and the fairies, reflected in the colour scheme of black and gold for the court and white, silver and gold for the fairies. In 1976 this concept was very evident, with the forest costumes and the fairies being negatives of the court costume. They were constructed differently; the court was more realistic and therefore used a lot of heavy boning and underpinnings, as well as heavier fabrics – brocades and velvets. The forest/dream costumes were constructed in a way that would make it easier for the actors to move – flexible boning rather than an equivalent to whalebone, crin petticoats rather than corded ones, or petticoats with hoops, and light sheer fabrics, especially silks. In 1976, when Jessica Tandy played Hippolyta/Titania, Titania's costume was the negative of her court Masque costume. She wore a solid Masque helmet with dragon for Hippolyta and a very transparent version of the helmet made out of crin, lace and found objects with the Titania costume.

Maggie Smith's interpretation of the role was quite different. Her Hippolyta became the old Elizabeth at the Court dreaming herself when she was younger; her Titania became the young Elizabeth before she came to the throne. This meant adjustments within the other characters' costumes – primarily the look of the Masque was changed. It used the same costumes but without headdresses. In 1977, Bottom's design changed to a more sexy look – Hume Cronyn in 1976 was a typical Elizabethan man, but Alan Scarfe in 1977 was more athletic in appearance. (SUSAN BENSON)

Susan Benson's designs for these two productions of A Midsummer Night's Dream embodied her view that the historical imagination was not readily accessible in late twentieth-century audiences as a means to guide their perception. Robin Phillips and Susan Benson were inspired by the paintings of the period to conceive tableaux as part of the visual aesthetic for the productions.[14] Rather than trying to evoke a period, she introduced into the costumes details that would be meaningful in the overall interpretation, the accretion of details attaining a metaphorical coherence.

The black, gold, and white palette of the productions was emblematic. Robin Phillips wanted the scenography to associate the play firmly with Queen Elizabeth I. Black and white contrasted reality and the dream – the Hippolyta and Titania aspects of Queen Elizabeth's reign – and gold figured the glory of her court. In 1976 the conceit was that of Elizabeth fantasizing herself and the Earl of Essex as a Hippolyta and Theseus, and her dream of them as Titania and Oberon. Benson's costumes made Jessica Tandy an earthbound Hippolyta and an ethereal Titania. The following season, with Maggie Smith playing Hippolyta/Titania as an Elizabeth musing on her youth and sexual adventures, Benson's costumes ceased to reflect the court in the forest. Instead, she endowed Hippolyta with majesty by different means, in consultation with Maggie Smith. Jewels sewn by hand onto the bodice of Hippolyta's costume signified royal opulence and served to make this court costume radiant when they were caught by the light, and they provided just the kind of detail that Benson likes to give her actors to work with. In 1977, Robin Phillips focussed audience attention on Hippolyta from the outset of the performance in a visual prologue. On the expanse of the Festival stage, Gil Wechsler's tightly focussed light picked out the bejewelled Hippolyta in her black velvet court dress with Philostrate at her feet. This silently created portrait of a Queen Elizabeth in the guise of Hippolyta was an image etched in the imagination of the spectators for the rest of the performance.

Benson's design also drew attention to the choreography. The costumes for the female characters emphasized the interplay of fabric and acting style, as did the cut of the costumes for the courtiers. For those Benson raised the trunk hose at the hip, thereby elongating the leg. This feature imparted an elegance to their movement that characterized this part of the mise en scène as balletic rather than realistic. The stark visual energy of the black and gold costumes together with the massiveness of this bare stage produced a stately monumentality. The actors worked in a scenically unmarked narrative space in which their presence invited intense interpretation by the spectators. The interplay between the realms of Hippolyta, the subjugated Amazon Queen, and Titania, the monarch of her own woodland realm, was largely realized through Benson's costume design.

Cabaret by Joe Masteroff and Fred Ebb, with music by John Kander (Stratford Festival, Festival Stage, 1987); *Guys and Dolls* by Abe Burrows and Joe Swerling with music by Frank Loesser (Stratford Festival, Festival Stage, 1990)

Cabaret suited the Festival Stage ideally in many ways, even though it was written for a proscenium stage – as are so many musicals – and it made moving from location to location, without interfering with the flow of the piece, very difficult to work out sometimes. It is a classic of its kind which you can interpret in a number of ways, and a piece which I would love to design again.

I love what Tanya Moiseiwitsch did with the Festival Stage. I have heard criticisms that it is dated, however, I think that it is like a piece of antique furniture which must be respected. I think that you have to build out from it, linking in some way the architectural details – either colour, tonal value, texture, or shape. At least one of these elements should link to the basic. In the case of *Guys and Dolls* I wanted to give the feel of a newspaper and to me fire escapes offered not only different levels, which Brian Macdonald loves to use, but also identified New York. They also allowed for easy transitions into different scenes. I kept the values dark and the set shapes reflected the angularity of the permanent stage. I think that it gave a totally different look to the permanent stage without fighting it.

The shape of the stage requires very careful proportions both in the set and in the clothes. The audience's attention is so focussed that you cannot let your attention to detail waver for a minute. This does not mean that a piece has to be overlain with detail and, in fact, some of the more successful designs on the stage were done by Daphne Dare, who tended to keep her designs very simple. The Festival stage forces you to give the attention to the actor and if you over-design you are fighting both the stage and the actor.

Guys and Dolls was the first musical on the stage that really required a 'Broadway Musical' approach. Given the design of the space, I do not think that a totally realistic interpretation would have worked. I used a very tight colour palette which was expanded only when they went to Cuba. I had originally intended to do it in black and white, i.e., the newspaper theme, but Brian Macdonald wanted colours so I played with the basic tonal values with touches of different shades of red, gold, also different shades of brown. (SUSAN BENSON)

With productions of *Cabaret* and *Guys and Dolls* Benson had to accommodate the Festival Stage to the idioms of Broadway musical for the first time.[15] Benson's design for *Cabaret* applied the principles used for the production of Shakespeare and used the costumes to provide a source of structure for this musical. At the close of Act 1 Benson shifted the colour scheme radically from the shimmering world of glamour of the Kit Kat Club to a prescient one of the more mundane fruit shop. For this scene of an engagement party set in Herr Schultz's fruit shop Benson chose a subdued palette with accents of colour evident in the patterning of the fabric and introduced a sense of 'make-do' in the details of the props for characters who appeared in both locations. She pointed to the fashion of the period but with a colour scheme that prompted the director to remark how the costumes articulated an as yet unspoken narrative: 'Susan had arrived at an extraordinary colour palette for the scene: blacks, greys, browns, creams, fawns and khakis: cloche hats and plus-fours, checkered sweaters and tweeds – each character and individual was etched in the latest fad of those months. But the scene was one of premonition, it showed us rot, a decadent demi-monde unknowingly doomed, fiancées that would never marry, a morality and thus a nation already ruptured ... As the singers and dancers played unawareness, and the trap closed, Susan made every visual detail telling, exact and appropriate to the closest scrutiny.'[16] The design of this production brought the focus on the stage forward and away from an emphasis on physical location.

For *Guys and Dolls,* Benson's scenography made no attempt to replicate the proscenium arch that the piece assumes. Instead, she ingeniously opened up for use the immense height of the Festival Theatre so as to replace the depth that can be achieved with a proscenium perspective. This emphasis on verticality also served to differentiate sharply the acting space of this production from the customary Shakespeare productions using the width of the stage. Benson built up a cityscape on the upstage wall with a series of platforms linked by stairs – like New York fire escapes – and she masked the permanent wooden stage structure with neon and painted signs between platforms, creating an impression of a street. This vertical configuration effectively conjured up the exciting, threatening milieu of the pedestrians in cavernous streets, much as a painter might. Scenes to be played 'in the city' were set on the fire escapes, which Michael Whitfield's lighting brought into sharp relief as called for, and allowed to recede into a general perspective when the floor space was used. Throughout the design Benson reconfigured the concepts of depth by emphasizing verticality. The conventional view of New York skyscrapers on a backcloth was transposed into a floor cloth, painted in forced perspective. This device was engagingly novel: since this downstage area of the theatre inverted the experience of rubbernecking a skyscraper, the spectators looked down on actors superimposed on the buildings. This image of skyscrapers on the floor cloth also made for energetic juxtapositions of proportions and planes. The painted skyscrapers and the three-dimensional fire escapes immediately set up the actors as controlling presences moving between the different planes and scales. By transforming the spatial characteristics of the Festival Theatre, Benson introduced the spectators to an unusually graphic scenography.

The choice of fabric for this production was particularly at issue. Benson often sought contemporary equivalents of materials that would be redolent of the 1950s. The balance in colour of the costumes allowed their cut to be simpler. The more vivid colours for the women were matched by checks and pinstripes for the men's suits. Together these costumes announced a period style. Benson's perseverance in creating meaningful details for the actors to work with on stage is evident in the particularization of one of the suits – she found a suitably evocative lining by integrating part of a modern-day suit from a local mall. Once again, Benson's device provided the actor, Peter Donaldson, with a unique detail that could be used in the development of a character.

The Mikado by W.S. Gilbert with music by Arthur Sullivan (Avon Theatre, 1982, 1983, 1984, Royal Alexandra Theatre, 1986, Avon Theatre, 1993, and tour National Arts Centre, Royal Theatre, Victoria, Living Arts Centre, Mississauga, 1998)

As I had not worked with Brian Macdonald[17] before, I did a series of thumbnail sketches for him. He said that he would like the piece to be flexible, with constantly changing locations, and beautiful. He did not want a two-set show such as the D'Oyly Carte Company had used up until this time. It had just come out of copyright. Luckily he liked the sketch that I was most attached to, which was my 'lily pad' idea.

I did not try to make it an authentic Japanese design. (This was also the case with *Madama Butterfly* for the Canadian Opera Company 1990.) I always do a lot of research on shows so that I have a good basis and then I try to put it away and add my own visions to the worlds I create. Both *Mikado* and *Madama Butterfly* were interpretations by Westerners and I think that it would not have served either piece to be too literal. (SUSAN BENSON)

Susan Benson has designed five Gilbert and Sullivan productions, of which her *Mikado* is the best known.[18] The inclusion of these musicals in the Stratford repertoire was a departure by John Hirsch in 1981 – a bold one, since there was no precedent at Stratford for musical theatre on such a scale.[19] The production was originally mounted during the 1982 season and it remained part of the regular repertoire for the next two seasons; subsequently, in 1986, the production toured the United States and seven years later it was revived at Stratford. In Toronto in 1998 it was revived once again for a national tour.

Abandoning the traditions of the D'Oyly Carte,[20] Susan Benson's designs for *The Mikado* took advantage of the black box stage of the Avon Theatre and only gradually added elements of moveable and flexible scenery. Seven oval 'lily pads,' manoeuvred on silent casters over the gold-tiled floor, connoted miniature stages in themselves, introducing a variety of visual rhythms and gently reconfiguring the geometry of the sight lines. Set in a sequence the pads looked like large stepping stones and if arranged by height they created a stairway, so that the focal point on the stage was easily altered by the choice of a lily pad and its height and placement on stage. These 'floating' scenes could be choreographed as a physical equivalent to a spotlight. Benson also introduced a great painted fan upstage, a piece of *Japonisme* that was as frank as it was highly theatrical in its scale.[21] This device of the scenographic fan declared the European origin and aestheticization of images of old Japan. The design of the costumes embodied a fresh, late twentieth-century *Japonisme* that knowingly exaggerated the embroidered kimono in its references to art nouveau, as Benson's design made no claim to continuity with any real or supposed Japan.

The sketches for this production vary in purpose and media in telling ways. For the details of the costumes Benson used watercolours with a precise sense of the nuance that the costume was to effect on stage – the long train, or the reshaping of the head by a wig or headdress. By contrast, Benson used pencil and pastels in the sketches for the makeup.[22] The crucial differentiation between the media in the sketches was that of texture, and shows how Benson fashioned the faces of the actors into masks. For the Mikado and the Gentlemen of Japan, Benson designed a face the eyebrows of which reiterated the strong horizontal line of the shoulders of the costume to point up the expanded body shape as part of the hierarchies of power. The concept of the makeup for the female characters was less indebted to the mask, apart from Katisha, for whom Benson not only designed elaborate facial makeup and created a more extreme head-dress than for the other women, but whose costume, by Benson's use of colour combinations, drew attention to its composition (in a way similar to what she had done for the male costumes to make them imposing silhouettes on stage). Together these details of the design illustrated the interplay of power and love in a commanding and articulate manner.

Eight years later, when Benson designed *Madama Butterfly* for the Canadian Opera Company (1990, 1994, 1998) her scenography evoked the imagery of a Japanese woodblock print and the functionality of Kabuki or Nō stage architecture. The design modified the proscenium stage of the Hummingbird Centre by the addition of a thrust stage – two European forms – but their structure and colour conveyed foreignness. The audience found itself in a cultural space between the familiar world of Puccini's opera and the otherness of staging. The enormous platform, with its clean lines and wood construction, was reminiscent of Japanese *theatre*. The step around the periphery of the platform broke up the architectural lines of the Hummingbird stage and allowed actors to be noticed as they came onto the stage, as they might be on the Japanese *hanamichi* of the Kabuki, or *hashigakan* of the Nō stages. Onstage/off-stage conventions were thus clearly differentiated from those mostly used in the proscenium theatre. Benson's design was a stylistical departure from the stage traditions of *Butterfly*, notably in its refusal of visual representation of old Japan, which has so often dominated the scenography. Puccini's romantic *Japonisme* clashed with the coolness and intensity of this modified Japanese *theatrical* aesthetic, effecting a performative collision of two cultures. The muted tones of the women's costumes and the scenographic structure, reinforced by Michael Whitfield's gentle, muted lighting, had the effect of flattening the perspective, much as in a Japanese woodblock print, thereby denying the spectator the splendour of many productions but heightening the intensity of the female tragedy.

Susan Benson's designs for opera and ballet are often hybrids of art forms. For instance, Benson's scenography for *The Marriage of Figaro* at the Banff Centre for the Arts in 1990 exploited subjects of neoclassical romantic painting and its two-dimensionality as powerful visual metaphors. Architecture and interior decor constituted a referential framework so that Count Almaviva's castle had walls, doorways, an elaborate cornice, and even garden statues, but Benson used landscape painting to narrate the action, rather than employing architectural interiors for that purpose. The scenography could be said to have reframed the action as an animation of pictorial representations. For each act Benson provided images redolent of a tradition of landscape painting, drawing on Corot, Fragonard, and Watteau for the design of inserted pieces, which declared themselves as such, used as upstage walls. For the first act, the upstage wall was dominated by an image of nymphs bathing in a forest pool being glimpsed by a hidden figure. This was reminiscent of Jean Baptiste Camille Corot's vistas of the forest at Fontainbleau, or his more allegorical *Diana Surprised by Actaeon*. For Act Two, the woodland scene of the wall was interrupted by a window embrasure but, nevertheless, the two nymphs took up the central focus. For Act Three, the stage opened into the drawing room with two large double doors to the gardens, but the paintings displayed a long vista into the forest, and on stage left the two bathing nymphs in the distance had turned their back to the spectator.[23] Finally, in Act Four, the nymphs of earlier scenes were realized as statuary in the garden. This final panel is reminiscent of *Le Surprise* by Fragonard, in which the lovers are discovered at the base of a statue of Cupid in the garden. Benson's design was a lively theatrical commentary on such compositions and animated the human figures against the backdrop of forest and statuary in the three dimensions of the stage. The costumes for the production (sketched in watercolours) were period, the period coming to life, as it were, within the pictorial composition.

Romeo and Juliet by John Cranko (National Ballet of Canada, Hummingbird Centre, 1995; National Ballet of Finland, 1996)

Some people may have been disappointed to begin with because they were used to Jürgen Rose's more colourful designs.[24] However, I did come to it with a very strong background in Shakespeare. I adore the music but I approached it in the same way as I would the play, wanting to make a fresh approach and make the drama very strong. It was difficult to change the overall look as the choreography does not allow for the downstage space to be encroached upon. You have to allow room for a certain number of dancers – the ball scene requires a certain number of couples in rows. The choreography calls for the bridge with stairs in certain scenes. Another thing that affects how you design the space is the length of the music. Budget also had a bearing on how scene changes, set pieces etc. were designed. I saw the ballet as a sombre piece with the two young lovers floating within this world. I wanted to give a feeling of the cruelty of their lives, that it had happened before and it would happen again. During the time that I was designing the piece there had been a case of two young people from different backgrounds being killed in Sarajevo. (SUSAN BENSON)

Benson's commission from the National Ballet Company for the design of *Taming of the Shrew* (1992) and *Romeo and Juliet* (1995) forged a new link between ballet choreography and scenography in Canada. John Cranko had choreographed both ballets as bold experiments in dance drama and Benson had experience designing for dance and dancers in Shakespearean and other productions at the Festival Theatre. Her designs for *Taming of the Shrew* referred to the Stratford stage in a self-conscious manner. An upper gallery spanning the width of the stage could be accessed by stairs, angled like elbows, from the stage floor. Beneath the gallery, the wall was punctuated by a series of arches that could be arranged to span the width of the stage, or reduced to only three between the staircases. The overall effect was reminiscent of Moiseiwitsch's Stratford stage. Benson rejected scene-painting of mortar and stone, choosing to give this imposing structure the appearance of a pastel rendering. The set functioned architecturally as stage space, but it also made the upstage construction into an artist's rendering, introducing visual expressiveness into the backdrop for the balletic action.[25]

Cranko's choreography for *Romeo and Juliet* is characterized by his attention to the world around the tragedy. His insistence on milieu is most pronounced in the specific reference to crucial and tragic exchanges in the marketplace, the ballroom, the balcony, and on the bridge where the two lovers part. Benson's design was a visually complex Verona that delved into Cranko's insistence on the dynamic balance between the architectural elements and human presence. On the backdrop Benson presented an asymmetrical arrangement of buildings forming a corner of a square, rather than a single façade of one building. The perspective did not lead to a clearly discernible vanishing point; rather, it dissolved into the shadows created by the buildings. In front of this backdrop stood a bridge that spanned the width of the stage. The relationship between the two was crucial to evoking the atmosphere relevant to Cranko's choreography. Initially, in the scenes of the marketplace, the view of the bridge lined up with the backdrop, so that the apex of the bridge coincided with the highest towers of the building. Benson used the frame of the proscenium to 'obscure' the tallest rooftops from the spectator's view and thereby suggested that this square that contained the action did not allow a sufficient distance for a pedestrian to be able to get a view of all the buildings. For the balcony scene and the final parting *pas de deux* Benson used the bridge alone against the cyclorama, saturated in a deep blue of night by Robert Thomson's lighting design, to bring the figures on the bridge into greater relief. By removing the backdrop she eliminated the urban context and used the bridge to suspend the lovers in time and place, adding to the poignancy of the story. Her design, which introduced a platform at the apex of the bridge – a space out of time – brought with it an important change in the choreography.[26] This step in the structure interrupted the visual rhythm of the arc of the bridge in a manner foreboding ill.

Benson's choice of a monochromatic palette for the backdrop, using greys and blues to reinforce the sense of stolid masonry, made it seem much more like an ink drawing or an engraving. Her initial sketches for the set had been done in ink, in earth tones, and gradually she brought these colours into the costumes themselves. Benson's palette for the costumes was opulent, especially against the grey and blue of the architectural details. The costumes picked up the grey, green, cream, strong orange, and red tones with the effect of intensifying the emotion, rather than depicting a period.[27] The ballerinas' overskirts and underskirts were of different colours, and in very light fabric, so that the colours were both revealed by motion and emphasized by it. With the focus on torso and arms necessary for a dancer, Benson's costumes nevertheless embodied dramatic values. For the ballroom scene, Benson designed a near fiery combination of costumes that momentarily changed the possibilities of the dancer's art. Juliet's costume consisted of a coat made of taffeta in orange and yellow with a stiff collar that framed her face. On her head she wore a tight jewel-encrusted cap that glittered in the light. Romeo's silhouette was also changed for the occasion – he wore a large cape with a train that extended about two feet behind him. Created in burnt orange with metallic accents, this cape too had a stand-up collar that framed his face and appliqué leaves around the neckline and on the back. By removing the cape Romeo effortlessly changed his shape, and therefore the way the spectators would perceive him – on stage he could transform himself from a formal, emblematic figure into a dancer. The costume for Tybalt was less elaborate but also offered two silhouettes – a tight black bodice was set off by long flowing sleeves, accented by gold braid and orange appliqué in the details. These costumes provided spectators with a means of identifying the Shakespearean characters and also the figures of a complex choreography. Benson's design was a carefully deliberated mediation between the balletic and the dramatic.

3

MARY KERR

'Theatre is what my family did for a living. "Art" is what I wanted to do – I wanted to be a sculptor, or an architect. Somehow, somewhere the two came together.'[1] Her mother's dance and theatre school in Winnipeg, along with hours spent in the wings of vaudeville houses and high school gyms while her mother adjudicated performances, left an indelible mark of theatricality on Mary Kerr. After formal training in painting and sculpture at the University of Manitoba[2] and a year towards an MA in applied design at the University of Waterloo, she switched to graduate studies at the University of Toronto in the fall of 1967. While she studied medieval art and literature there she also began to design for the Poculi Ludique Societas,[3] for other theatre groups in Toronto and Waterloo, and for shows for young audiences. Her professional career was thoroughly launched with *The Stag King* at the Tarragon Theatre in December 1972.

Mary Kerr has designed for theatre, dance, opera, musical review/cabarets, and film. Some of her stage designs have been for smaller venues, such as the Tarragon, Kaleidoscope (at the Belfry), Toronto Free Theatre, Buddies in Bad Times (Poor Alex), Phyzikal Theatre (Theatre Centre), Theatre in the Dell, the Hour Theatre Company, and Studio Lab; others have been for such theatres as the Grand Theatre, Young People's Theatre, Canadian Stage (St Lawrence Centre), Vancouver Playhouse, the National Arts Centre, and those at the Shaw and Stratford Festivals.[4] She has also designed opera, for the Canadian[5] and the Vancouver Opera Companies,[6] as well as at Mercury Theatre in Auckland, New Zealand;[7] dance, for the Royal Winnipeg[8] and Ontario Ballet[9] Companies; and several cabaret and musical revues.[10] One of her most important collaborators has been dancer Danny Grossman, with whom she developed performances for fifteen years (between 1976 and 1991). Between 1977 and 1982 she worked at CBC Television and on several feature films. Kerr's extra-theatrical design projects also include *The*

Goose and Beaver Show, an on-site entertainment at the Canadian Pavilion at Expo '86 in Vancouver, and, for the XVth Commonwealth Games held in Victoria in 1994, the logo, uniforms, and signage as well as the impressive opening and closing ceremonies. She has been awarded seven Dora Mavor Moore, Jessie Richardson, and Sterling Awards for set and costume design, and her designs for *The Desert Song* (Shaw Festival, 1982) were part of the Canadian showcase sent to the Prague Quadrennial in 1983. In 1996 she was elected to the Royal Canadian Academy of the arts. She has taught at Ryerson Polytechnic Institute, the University of Waterloo, York University, and the University of Victoria. Currently she combines professional commissions with a full-time appointment to the department of theatre at the University of Victoria.

The Stag King by Carlo Gozzi, adapted by Sheldon Rosen (Tarragon Theatre, 1972)

> The production was intended to be stylized in the period of the sixteenth century, adapted to the conditions of the Tarragon (for example: no backstage space to store flats, no fly gallery, a ceiling height of 14' and a concrete floor). The design solution is a false proscenium stage, with a smaller stage inside. Painted drops on curtain rods for each scene are pulled apart by hand to reveal the next scene. Painted around the inner stage are people in theatre boxes as if watching the performance. The figures have Christmas tree bulbs for eyes, which flash whenever a magic spell is being used. The set is white with black outlines ... The show curtain is a large zodiac.[11] (MARY KERR)

The scenography for the second season at the Tarragon (formerly an electronics factory) was eclectic. Abstraction prevailed in the split stage for Tremblay's *Forever Yours, Marie Lou*, designed by Gary Wagner and Dan Yahri, and realism in the re-mount of French's *Leaving Home*, designed by Dan Yahri and Stephen Katz. Mary Kerr's design was a third scenographic variation: she transformed the Tarragon into a miniaturized and idiosyncratic version of a Renaissance court stage. Her stylization of designs by Inigo Jones adapted their perspective geometry to provide an illusion of a much greater space. A bold checkerboard pattern painted directly on the cement floor accentuated the sense of depth, while the line drawings in the false proscenium opening, set well upstage, converged on contemporary cartoon style. Kerr exploited the proximity of the upstage façade and infused it with a carnivalesque humour: instead of the statuary that might have graced a Renaissance proscenium or *scaena* she inserted an outline drawing of a figure striking a grand pose with the face and the hands cut out, so that an actor stepped into the 'statue.' Again, the fictive patrons in the 'theatre boxes' were depictions of Tarragon personnel, the Marx brothers, and her parents.

Kerr's costumes also played boldly with the historical period, as her sketches show. Done in felt-tip markers on large cardboard mats (15 in. × 20 in.) these sketches investigate the possibilities of colour. The colour scheme for the costumes was allegorical: black and white to distinguish good characters from evil ones; purple for the selfishly stupid; yellow for the truthful and joyful; the rainbow reserved for the magical.[12] The silhouettes of the costumes self-consciously straddled various periods: the exaggerations of *commedia dell'arte* are evident in the sketch for Smeraldina with its endless bows and tucks; the design for Clarissa, by contrast, harked back to the Ballets Russes, and especially Natalia Gontcharova's modifications of Russian folk motifs,[13] while for the characters such as Cigolotti and Derandarte, fitted out in rainbow colours, the tones of the early 1970s were superimposed on Renaissance form, and Cigolotti, a storyteller, was figured as an elaborate representation of a bird. For this production (in contrast with the other shows of that Tarragon season) the spectators were positioned outside the performance to read the codes of a theatre altogether different in scale and style from this converted factory.

Nothing Sacred by George F. Walker, based on **Fathers and Sons** by Ivan Turgenev (CentreStage, Bluma Appel Theatre, St Lawrence Centre, 1988, and a co-production tour by the National Arts Centre and Citadel Theatre, 1989)

Frank Lloyd Wright's encouragement to liberate oneself from the tyranny of the box has always guided my designs. In *Nothing Sacred* I started by realigning the squared opening of the proscenium and letting the design flow into the auditorium using the pine floorboards in forced perspective like a river of wood. The challenge was to find a governing metaphoric landscape to support the many locations – Russian forests, rolling landscapes, and interiors. To reach beyond a simple picture of a place in the theatre I used doorways held by the asymmetrical forced perspective of canvas walls (decreasing in size from 16' downstage to 5' upstage) to set the limits of the fields and also to open the stage emotionally. The return walls were made of transparent material lit for each scene change to mirror psychologically with colour and kinetic action Alain Laing's brilliant sound design.

The show began downstage, a graphic wooden forest cut-out proscenium curtain that invited you to look through it to the stage beyond. The trees were made of four types of unpainted layered wood, to invite the question of what is organic. For interiors, the small back wall with an unframed door flew down to complete the 'box set.' For exteriors, the back wall flew and we brought in flat graphic cutouts of pine and birches which were influenced by folk imagination and Bilibin's illustration of Russian folk tales.[14] (MARY KERR)

With the scenography for *Nothing Sacred* in 1988 Mary Kerr embarked on a re-examination of the proscenium stage. She drew much of her inspiration from the concept of 'organic' architecture articulated by Frank Lloyd Wright.[15] Kerr applied Wright's dual principles of continuity and plasticity to her own scenography in order to integrate structural and aesthetic aspects of design. The preliminary drawings and maquettes constitute a record of the stylistic negotiations Kerr conducted between the philosophical nihilism of the protagonist, Bazarov, and the fecundity of the Russian forest and countryside. The rawness of the first maquette is particularly telling: an undulating landscape, modelled in plasticine, shaped into a forced perspective, with a stage floor that flows off the edge of the stage into the auditorium, like lava. As for the nihilism, it finds its analogue in the room of translucent paper surrounding the landscape. Against the lively rhythms of the floor and the perspective Kerr inserts cut-outs of hand-drawn trees to stand in for Russian forests. Here, Kerr deliberately confuses the two-dimensionality of illustrations and three-dimensionality of human experience. A second maquette further explores the visual rhythms that will result from the use of specific materials. The false proscenium adds a twist to the blond planks of the rake, while the plywood cut-outs of trees engage the spectator in two distinct perspectives: they naively deny distance, like Bilibin's illustrations, while the stage floor accelerates, as it were, the movement of the eye over the landscape.

On Kerr's set the actors had to perceive and use the set rhythmically, almost like dancers, to appreciate themselves as figures in relation with the design elements, rather than with the fiction place. Entrances through the upstage area or through the doorways presented the figures, at first view, as silhouettes, to which costumes derived from the style of the period added visual interest. A certain abstract quality of the scenography allowed simultaneous and harmonizing rhythms in the setting of furniture in the several flat areas provided for it – chairs for a porch, a Persian rug for a mid-stage interior, a large table set at the lip of the stage for a dining room. Such accommodation for various settings without major set changes was in keeping with Wright's interplay between interior spaces and the external definition of whole building.

A final element was Alain Lortie's lighting in this scenography. Kerr cast lighting as a major design element; using scrim in the returns for the seven doorways she was able to illuminate these walls in various colours to emphasize specific moments. This synaesthetic scenography merged the characters' 'psychological truths, [and] insights'[16] with the spectators' reading of objective realities on stage.

The Three Penny Opera by Bertolt Brecht, music by Kurt Weill (Banff Centre for the Arts and Canadian Stage, Bluma Appel Theatre, St Lawrence Centre, 1989)

This set is a merging of my own extensive investigation of the sculptural quality of abandoned industrial sites and my fascination with the designs of the Russian Constructivists. While doing the preliminary designs I kept always in mind two epigrammatic statements: 'the actor is the man at the border between reality and fantasy,' by Erwin Piscator, and 'the art of the actor is to expose life not represent it' by Max Reinhardt.[17] I choose to shift the rules of perspective so that there would be no one fixed point of view. I have used a spiral or circle in many designs because it allows for a dynamic choreography as the set becomes a gigantic sculpture. The spiral can be found in every culture and the prominence of the circle in theatre architecture is equally present in ancient Greek theatres and in contemporary stadiums. Standing at the very centre of such a circle is empowering. However, in *The Three Penny Opera* I created a deconstructed circle: broken, twisted, distorted, spiralling off in the third dimension parallelling the disorienting quality of life now. The musical director in costume and white face hung suspended over the stage conducting the orchestra and the actors below: like some Mephistopheles or Weill. I attempted to reflect the rhythms of Weill's music in the structures of the costumes and the sets. (MARY KERR)

Kerr's scenography for *The Three Penny Opera* sought to dismantle the pictorial perspective of a proscenium arch. She chose to break up the expectation of continuous space by a scenography that eschewed a flat floor and consisted rather of a multilevel stage installation. The result was a fractured space that realigned, much like a cubist painting, as a series of expressive slanted planes, ramps, and catwalks that consciously pointed to the volume of the space, rather than its depth. The actors in this environment had to develop a vocabulary for the stage that was gestural, kinetic, and highly visual.

She embarked on the scenography for *The Three Penny Opera* by creating a photographic record of unused industrial sites on Granville Island in Vancouver and at the Gooderham and Worts Distillery in Toronto. Isolating architectural elements from their functional contexts, she revealed an intricate abstract or geometric aesthetic of corrugated metal, rusted grille-work, boarded-up windows, and rivetted metal.[18] She integrated some of these images with quotations from Constructivist sculpture and architecture. Her preliminary sketches reflect the compression of industrial space with a head-on view of a courtyard between two factory façades. To this, she added a wrought iron spiral through the central section, onto which the title of the play would be 'welded.' She rejected this initial volumetric organization of the space as she abstracted the architectural elements from her photos. The final scenography was a stage collage of fire escapes, metal bridges, sluices, and catwalks arranged around a large oval ramp. The walls, which might have created a forced perspective, were set at distinctly incompatible angles: the stage right wall appeared to be twisted under a dynamic strain, while the stage left wall looked like a portable scenic façade with its corner resting in an audience box, awaiting its next installation, as it were. Moreover Kerr obliterated the impression of a fixed right-angled proscenium arch when she inserted false structural beams (which resembled many of the architectural aspects of the set), to engender ambiguity between an impression of industrial architecture and the unmasking of the actual structure of the theatre itself. For her first maquette, she designated canvas and plywood as the main construction materials and used colour sparingly – off-white, ivory, rust red, and black – to achieve a bleached appearance,[19] but for the actual set she deliberately juxtaposed wood and 'metal,' demonstrating their qualities of construction in these abstract assemblages.[20] Kerr paired elements created in one plane with those in another, altering the scale to invite contemplation of the visual rhythms: the sewer cover, located at the upstage edge of the platform, was a miniaturized version of the moon, and the construction of both repeated the exposed lathe on the building. These details created a visual energy independent of the actors. The immediate effect was to make the spectator very conscious of the way in which the set had been constructed, and a less evident aspect was the skill demanded of the stage carpenters in the realization of this design.[21]

Kerr drew attention specifically to the lighting and sound. She considered illumination from within the set, as through the 'metal' grille near the base of the oval which could be lit from underneath to cast intricate shadows on the actors. She also ignored the theatre's orchestra pit when she extended the set into the auditorium. The musicians were relocated to the fly gallery, seen through the window cut-outs, and the conductor entered in a gondola from the flies, to remain there in the full view of the spectators. This scenography foregrounded the available technology and claimed with Piscator and Reinhardt a central role for scenographic expression.

The red, white, and black colour scheme of the costumes and the placement on stage of their wearers introduced another pattern of organization into the production. In effect, given the shape of the set, the figures are 'showcased' as sculpted images of social interaction. Sketches show each costume with its own idiosyncratic patterning of textures and colours[22] and often the name of the character is stencilled on a sleeve or a leg.[23] Kerr pairs her sketches of individual costumes so as to emphasize the importance of stage composition of figures in her scenographic conception. For the Gang, she creates clownesque costumes, with one trouser leg and one leotard leg, and with buttons to outline the seams. Her beggars have their slogans written on the costumes – an extension of the 'literarization' called for by Brecht. The right side of Macheath is costumed like a dancer, with a leg in red with black stripes and a form-fitting vest, while his left side is a more formally suited, but with no shirt to his collar and cuffs. Tiger Brown and Jeremiah Peachum are paired up to show not only the distinctions made by their costumes but also where the colour accents of red are to appear and how the marks of office are to be manifested – Brown wears his medals on his sleeve, has an imposing moustache, and a great coat that exaggerates his silhouette, while Peachum is a jumble of fashions with a highly tailored coat. Polly has a whole design card to herself. Her costumes parody those of respectable society and, except for the last one to be worn, defy the overall colour scheme. Altogether the effect of Kerr's scenography was to separate Brecht's text from the particular presentational artefact.

If We Are Women by Joanna McClelland Glass (a co-production Vancouver Playhouse, 1993, Canadian Stage, 1994)

The scenography for this production sought to create a visual bridge/frame to listen to four women talk about Life, Love, and Aging. The wooden floor, in forced perspective, was adrift in an emotional sea of silk. The furniture and characters on the abstracted home/raft seemed recognizable to us all but floating in a brain/womb of fabric. The extensive use of fabric surrounded the women's observations and memories in a stage environment of sculptural transparency. Originally I thought that the cloth aspects of the set (water, walls and clouds) would be lit in various colours and gobos to register the complex emotional reactions of the characters. Eventually, it was only the walls of the set that reacted to the women, while the silk water that surrounded the house moved gently throughout the play and the lighting shifts beneath it had a distinct visual rhythm. The proscenium curtain was *The Birth of Venus* by Botticelli, but with a New England lighthouse, cottage and sailboats behind. (MARY KERR)

Kerr's scenography made the dwelling into a kind of raft on which the young woman's sexual awakening is juxtaposed with the life experience of the three older women. The proscenium curtain gently parodied *The Birth of Venus* and set up the proportions of the painting as a point of reference. This spatial organization balanced the thematic concepts of generational memory set against the surrounding elements,[24] and weaned the spectators from the merely objective reality.

Kerr's preliminary sketches for the set show a process of abstraction. An early image outlines a 'cardboard cutout' boathouse of which the windows and doors all draw the eye of the spectators into the upstage area and make it seem mysterious. In many sketches the dock juts through the proscenium opening, complete with railing for added seating and stairs leading down into the auditorium. Through the series of sketches Kerr plays with the relative importance of the structure of the house in relation to two doorways (one functional and used as access to the second floor, and the other symbolic, designated for the male visitor). By shifting the emphasis away from the details of the house (roof, walls, and windows) in the various versions Kerr eventually reverses the relationship between the walls and the sky. In the penultimate sketch she paints the walls as a sky, and leaves staircases to descend surrealistically to the main platform; she replaces the roof with a ceiling of light puffy clouds. Her completed design brings back the idea of walls, but makes them the focus for a complex light show, which underscores the emotional narrative of the play and creates a visual image of femaleness.

Bella Judy Jarvis Dance Company (Dance Umbrella, New York City, 1977)

Danny [Grossman], Judith [Jarvis] and I studied Chagall paintings and drawings to assimilate the body angles, hand gestures, colours and delicate magic of the Chagall dream. Many of his paintings have the lover in flowers, or over horses – really special worlds of their own. The problem was to convey the style of a master by not copying, but yet echoing him. Particularly hard for me as Chagall has always been close to my heart.[25] (MARY KERR)

Kerr's scenography for *Bella* came soon after a year's study (supported by an Artist's Grant from the Canada Council) of design for dance. Her notebooks from that year are filled with observations about the differences between the relationship of a designer with a dancer/choreographer and with a theatre director. While she had investigated theatrical analogues to visual and sculptural art when working with Stephen Katz,[26] when it came to dance she rethought the balance between visual presentation and the exigencies of the choreography. With respect to costumes, she sought to fulfil the need for flexibility and stretch in the fabric by painting or dying leotards as part of her own research about colour and composition.

In 1975 she began her collaboration with Danny Grossman, an artistic relationship that spanned fourteen productions. Her costumes for *National Spirit* (1976) combined leotards with vividly coloured dance briefs and vests for the highly athletic choreography.[27] For *Fratelli* (1976) the costumes for the two male dancers were mirror images of each other, incorporating such pieces as a dyed white calf and a separate cuff worn by each dancer. The set for this choreography comprised a painted panelled screen of four storybook backgrounds, against which the dancers became figures in an illustration. Occasionally Kerr subtitles her designs: *The Party* (National Ballet of Canada, 1977) was 'Colour in Motion Kinetic Sculpture'[28] because she used a costume colour to characterize each figure in the narrative. By the early 1990s the costumes were being used to superimpose a collage on the revealed body of the dancer,[29] so that in *Ecce Homo* (1990) for Danny Grossman she used netting to replace what in earlier costumes might have been a block of solid-coloured fabric.[30]

Bella (1977) was an important work that brought together painting, sculpture, costume, and set design with dance. The project took as its point of departure the fascination with Marc Chagall that Danny Grossman, Judy Jarvis, and Mary Kerr shared – Chagall's paintings of circuses and lovers and the biographical details of the painter's love for his wife, Bella. Kerr was involved in the development of the piece from the early stages, sketching her designs as the dancers rehearsed and serving as the outside eye to see if the dance had the 'feel of the painting.' Kerr subtitled this design 'Lovers in Violet'[31] and considered the dance a 'living sculpture'[32] since it so fully incorporated the 'set' – a horse derived from Chagall's paintings.

The costume sketches in coloured pencil on blue mat reflect Kerr's appreciation for the painter's compositions and sense of colour, his layering of images and textures of paint. Her dancers' bodies similarly appear to float on the page. In colour and form, their leotards are a continuation of the garden setting, poised between clothing and scenery. The horse was developed on the model of Chagall's naive images of circus scenes. During rehearsals hand- and footholds, as well as padding, were added to the basic wooden structure and later masked by the dense floral pattern. The support provided by the horse allowed the choreography to approximate the weightlessness in the paintings. In the first half of the dance the two dancers were lovers floating under the bower of flowers, remaining on the horse and only occasionally touching the ground; in the second half of the dance the horse remained upstage of the dancers as they descended to the floor, as to a public world, and it was only upon Bella's death and ascent into heaven that the dancers returned to the horse. The scenography for this dance provided physical equivalents for a timeless painterly metaphor of love and the highly temporal three-dimensionality of figures in the world.

Zurich 1916 by John Bentley Mays, with music by Christopher Butterfield (Banff Centre for the Arts, 1998)

> This design draws on the cacophonous, hopeful, mad excitement of Dada and Cabaret theatre after the First World War, when costumes became part of the structure of the performance. Each costume was a commentary on the art and artists of the time – vibrant colours and forms coming out of the cabaret darkness. Although I had done a lot of work with other periods of the twentieth century, I had not yet had a chance to design a production from this period. Designing this show was a breakthrough for me – to find simple visual metaphors for rich complex ideas. This production was the beginning of my thinking about costumes as 'set design for the body' since each costume was a work of art, in a production that was an art show about the stage. (MARY KERR)

Mary Kerr's training in fine art and sculpture emerges in many of her designs[33] but nowhere as clearly as in *Zurich 1916*. For the costumes in the scenes of the Café Voltaire Kerr quoted Dada and Futurist art and the cabaret theatre of the time. Her compositions enacted the social impact of these art works in a lively, interrogative manner. *L'Oeil Cacodylate* (1916) by Francis Picabia, a montage of signatures and photos of the Dadists, became the fabric for the body suit of the 'Tattooed Lady,' while the costume for Tristan Tzara was reminiscent of Sonia Delaunay's simultaneous costumes.[34] Kerr created the 'Parade Horse' as a glancing reference to the costumes for the American and French managers in *Parade* designed by Pablo Picasso for the 'ballet réaliste'[35] by Jean Cocteau in 1916. She added her own variations on the popular entertainments of the early twentieth century in costumes such as that of the ballerina 'Marie,' whose tutu was a merry-go-round/mobile on which Kerr suspended tiny black and white images of the artists of the period, such as Hugo Ball in the paper costume of the Dada. The effect of these costumes was to mask the body of the performer and to create a performance of kinetic sculptures.[36]

In another scene Vsevolod Meyerhold's production of *Death of Tarelkin* was directly referred to in the figure of the animator of the chorus who wore a white coat bearing Meyerhold's name on the sleeve and the title of the play at the hem. The other actors in the scene wore stylized versions of the signature *prozodezhda* (loose-fitting workers' overalls) used by the designer Varvara Stepanova in 1922, on which Kerr had stencilled bits of Cyrillic text.[37] These costumes characterized the chorus of Russian people listening to V.I. Lenin's call for a national opera as the constructivist artists whose parodies of tsarist Russia worked out a physical and visual performance of politics.

XV *Commonwealth Games* (Opening Ceremonies, Victoria, 18 August 1994)

I see my stage designs as organic or architectural sculpture that are almost like 'installation pieces' in the theatre for the period of the run. If possible, I like to sit in the quiet of the empty theatre space and allow myself to feel not only the spatial dynamics but the actual living spirit within. It's not something I think of consciously, but nonetheless a response occurs. I mentally see design solutions in space, I then chop and change them as I sit there without actually drawing or modelling. It is the space, not just the stage that speaks to me and informs my designs. I see the theatre, whatever the scale, in the same friendly, comfortable way that I see my own studio. It is a place to dream and discover and share wonder.

So for the Games I had to think on several scales and detail and textures. The largest is for the picture of the Goodwill Blimp will have – The Busby Berkeley shot. The next, the close-up that the 36 cameras handheld, dollied and overhead sliding along the wires would have, and the third – the most traditional – what the audiences in the stands would see in this large theatre in the round.

There is the human scale, object scale, group scale, and then the sky scale. I made a stadium – gridded the floor and then began playing with pieces of paper and sculptures until it felt right. Stadium shows that only have human scale images work only for the television close-up. They really do not work. The possibilities and the medium are so very exciting. (MARY KERR)

Once upon a time, growing up in Winnipeg, Mary Kerr was a baton twirler and a Pink Bomberette, excited by the scales of productions in which she took part. The XV Commonwealth Games provided her with a great opportunity to work on yet a larger scale. Her design for the opening ceremonies exploited the size of the stadium and the various points of view from the stands and from the cameras. It was rooted not only in the internationalism of the Commonwealth Games but in the culture of the West Coast nations, and marked very clearly the site of the stadium on land formerly held by the Salish People.

The ceremonies, entitled 'The Spirit of Transformation,' were divided into five major segments. In the first sequence, more than 500 children ran onto the field carrying what appeared to be shields of various shapes and colours. Once they raised the shields over their heads the centrefield was transformed into an enormous decorative folk-art panel. The next installment brought a purely human scale as 340 lacrosse 'players' flooded onto the field. Kerr created sports costumes for them, for which the colour scheme for the right side was the mirror image of the left, alternating red and white. This design instantly created two teams, so that as the lines of dancers advanced upon each other a stylized game was effected. The third instalment of the ceremonies enacted the Legend of Kawaillika (the first man born of woman), which explains the different peoples of the world. For this, Kerr changed the scale radically: as she narrowed the focus to individual figures, she magnified their size and thereby instilled an epic quality in the presentation. In the prelude to the legend, Kerr began to change the scale. At first, long lengths of white fabric, decorated with red and black patterns of the West Coast Nations, were carried into the stadium, and as they fluttered in the breeze they resembled a flowing river. Above these turbulent waters birds (puppets on long rods) flew, while along the banks caribou[38] roamed. When the river was established in the centre field it filled with jumping salmon (soft sculpture puppets on long rods). The legend continued with the entrance the Wolf, an enormous puppet in the style of Bread and Puppet Theatre;

this figure was 25 feet wide and as many high, and depended for its form on a steel frame with a cloth covering which was decorated in a pattern derived from West Coast wood carvings. About ten people manipulated the head, and another twenty to thirty volunteers were responsible for moving the torso and articulating the paws to make the animal 'walk.' Kerr continued this enormous scale when this creature gave birth to four superhuman figures who were to live on the island created in the centre field. Each of these figures was about three to four times the height of its manipulators. The island itself was represented by four stylized evergreens. The final transformation of this sequence was a highly symbolic one: the outer dressing on these trees was removed to reveal four carved posts of a traditional Large House, at the same time as a painted façade of the building was being assembled. Elders from the various Native peoples came to the Large House and opened the Games, honouring the traditions of the Kwagiuthl and Salish Peoples who had inhabited this area of Vancouver Island. When Queen Elizabeth accepted the baton to declare the Games open, she did so with the Native Elders and the Large House as a backdrop.

The penultimate segment maintained the magnified scale but also opened the imagery to the international character of the Games. Eight dolls, each 26 feet high and 18 feet in diameter, were rolled onto the field. The dolls represented eight different areas of the world: India, the Northern Countries, the Mediterranean, the South Pacific and Polynesia, Eastern Europe, Africa, Asia, and the Caribbean and Latin America. Each doll was surrounded by dancers in costumes that were abstracted from the design on the skirt of the large figure. Once in place, these dolls with their dancers were joined on the field by 98 folk dancers from community groups in Victoria. The field was awash with diverse dance, before all the dancers on the field joined hands to circle round the dolls counterclockwise.

For the final segment, Kerr increased the size of the image by shifting from a vertical perspective of the first sequence of the petal people to a horizontal one. As the folk dancers moved to one end of the field, hundreds of volunteers dressed in white walked onto it. In a matter of moments they assembled in the shape of the white dove of peace holding an olive branch. The body took form when volunteers opened white umbrellas and the rainbow-coloured tail feathers opened when 40 runners broke away from the body, each unfurling 8-foot widths of fabric from their knapsacks to form the plumage. In a few minutes, the white umbrellas were replaced by grey ones and in the centre of the body of the bird a medallion of a Thunderbird emerged. At the same time 40 new runners stretched out lengths of grey cloth to complete the final image of the opening ceremonies, a Thunderbird that measured 70 feet wide and 215 feet long.

Mary Kerr designed these opening ceremonies as a magnificent local manifestation of multi-culturalism – with 3,000 volunteer participants on the field and no one scale of representation dominating the four-hour event she created a multi-focal view. She brought the energy and excitement of stadium shows with their resistance to only one point of view and the energy that comes from changing the scale of representation to enact these different kinds of narratives.

4

JIM PLAXTON

The high degree of integration of structure, sequence, movement, and lighting in Jim Plaxton's scenography is partly attributable to his familiarity with architecture, as well as with film and dance. During the early 1960s in Winnipeg, Plaxton worked in an architect's office, where he learned about space as 'volume and about the sculptural aspects of space ... what a space feels like when you walk into it.'[1] When he came to Toronto in 1965, Plaxton worked as a freelance architectural draftsman and, after studying film at The Three Schools of Art (1966–7),[2] started making 16mm films, as well as working at Film Canada (a small film distribution house) and Cinecity Theatre on Yonge Street. Intrigued by design and perception operating in 'real time and space,'[3] he began to experiment with design for performance. His first design was for the Toronto Dance Theatre at the MacMillan Theatre, where his stark, sculptural sets for *Encounter* (1969)[4] made a counter-rhythm to the lithe, angular choreography by Peter Randazzo. Another among his early theatre designs was *Treasure Island* (1974) for Studio Lab at the Bathurst Street Theatre.[5] Rather than the impassive, abstract forms he had created for dance, Plaxton here introduced found objects that he employed in distinctly different contexts to impart a visual structure to performance. These experiments in kinaesthetics and re-interpretation of objects for the stage are characteristic of Plaxton's approach to scenography, which he calls 'machines for acting' – an extension of the Modernist architectural tenet that houses are *'machines à habiter.'*[6] It is an apt enough motto for sets and lighting that furnish highly functional spaces for performance, but does not suggest the intense emotional qualities with which his scenography is also imbued. *The Crackwalker*, discussed below, is a characteristic example of such an emotive scenographic 'machine.'

Plaxton's volumetric approach to scenography – using height and depth in nonperspectival ways – has been a significant contribution to the adaptation of warehouses and other such spaces to performance, embracing the possibilities they offered of seeing and presenting in non-traditional ways. He has designed productions in many post-industrial venues: Global Village Theatre, Toronto Workshop Productions, Phoenix Theatre, Toronto Free Theatre (later Canadian Stage), Tarragon Theatre, Centaur Theatre, Bathurst Street Theatre, Native Earth Performing Arts, Adelaide Court, and the Theatre Centre. With very few exceptions the lighting design for these theatres is particularly difficult because many of them had – some still have – a lighting grid so low as to severely restrict the range of focal angles and lengths. His experiments primarily using light, such as those for *History of Village of the Small Huts* or *Prism, Mirror, Lens,* dispensed with a traditional model of area coverage from a grid and offered a fresh approach to design with light from different sources. He has also designed for more conventional theatrical venues such as the Guelph Spring Festival, the Court House Theatre at The Shaw Festival,[7] Adelaide Court Theatre, Hart House Theatre,[8] Factory Theatre (on Adelaide), and George Brown College. Outdoors, Plaxton's scenography for the Dream in High Park and Skylight Theatre in Earl Bales Park resembled on-site installations in that the structures took advantage of the given surroundings, using proportions related to the parkland sites. He is the winner of six Dora Mavor Moore Awards and represented Canada at the Prague Quadrennial in 1983. Although Plaxton has been associated with several theatre companies he remains a freelance designer.

In the early 1980s, Clarke Rogers, the new artistic director at Theatre Passe Muraille,[9] made Jim Plaxton an associate artistic director and together they conducted a complex experiment in performance. Plaxton's scenography in the unrenovated space[10] was often an architectural installation. The setting for *D + C* (1983)[11] was a one bedroom apartment that Plaxton realized, more or less, by a large platform (20 feet × 20 feet) suspended on three sides, with the standing walls made out of metal mesh. He added an extensive backstage annex so that the actors remained in a fictional apartment even when out of sight. The platform served as the living room and took on the connotations of a boxing ring when the arguments became violent. Plaxton devised a modified floor, cushioned with tires, that resonated as the couple fought. A backstage space included 'a heavy (lockable) "front door" which was the only access into the playing space, a working bathroom (the first ever in the building), and a double bed – to add an actor friendly location for the delivery of lines from the bed or bathroom as called for as "lines off" in the script' (Plaxton). The audience could imagine the invisible spaces whence sound came. The metal mesh that enclosed the platform was necessary to isolate the action from the audience and protect them from flying debris as the argument escalated,[12] but Plaxton also used it specifically for the lighting, drawing attention to its presence and thus wresting the scenography away from mere voyeurism. This design presented the audience with several concepts of space: the backspace functioned acoustically, the living room visually and acoustically, and the outlines of the room as the resonant casing for this acoustic instrument.

The Crackwalker by Judith Thompson (Centaur Theatre, 1982)

> The design challenge here was a play written with multiple and repeated locations presented on a fixed set. Scenes had to be 'cut' together, film-style. This was made possible by separating adjacent scenes in space rather than time. This would not be possible without carefully planned backstage traffic, allowing for easy and quick access to any part of the set. Any set should serve the actor. (JIM PLAXTON)

The scenography for *The Crackwalker* defined itself in the Centaur Theatre's smaller space (in a hall of the former Montreal Stock Exchange). Plaxton's design managed many scene changes, using a staircase with entrances directly onto the specific areas of the set, thereby minimizing the need for wing space so that the structure could exploit almost the full volume of the 36-foot width and the 20-foot height below the lighting grid. The staircase running through the centre divided the two halves of the stage, and connected all the scene locations both physically and visually. By arranging the locations vertically, with the Donut Shop at the top and the culvert for the Crackwalker directly below it, Plaxton realized a hierarchy implied in Judith Thompson's script. Between these locations was Sandy's apartment stage right and down the stairs from the Donut Shop, while Theresa's apartment was aligned more closely with the culvert in the nether regions, and thus was also below the Donut Shop on stage left. Sandy's apartment was presented as a naturalistic setting, visually associated with the Donut Shop. Theresa's apartment, set as it was next to the culvert, made associations with it, not only because the furnishings were makeshift, but because the space into the kitchen matched the culvert's disappearance into the unknown upstage. This spatial arrangement assured that no one space dominated, cut the running time of the play, and intensified the action. The audience saw the whole set when they walked into the theatre and it very quickly took on metaphorical implications – the Donut Shop became a haven/heaven and the culvert for the Crackwalker an abyss or hell mouth.

Moreover, Plaxton's set introduced an architectural geometry that brought with it a host of significant connotations. The contrast between enclosed and open spaces added to the emotional tension: Theresa's apartment could never evoke the sense of safety of Sandy's, with its full wall. Plaxton defined Theresa's space primarily by tightly controlled area lighting; it appeared to be more of a passage than a destination, and resembled the culvert in the way it opened to an off-stage space. For the excoriating scene in which the baby is placed in the oven, Plaxton linked the Donut Shop with Theresa's apartment by changing the spectators' lines of vision: the mirror of the Donut Shop was inclined, omnisciently and silently, to make the audience privy to the devastating scene below. Plaxton also matched the visual rhythm of the roundness of the culvert, as it opened 'into' the audience, with the circular form of tires stacked in Theresa's apartment. In the other direction the bars of the culvert also aligned with the treads of the staircase, seeming to expand the staircase ominously into the gutter. Plaxton's architectural structure constituted a free-standing stage with subtle kinaesthetic patterning.

O.D. on Paradise by Linda Griffiths and Patrick Brymer (Theatre Passe Muraille, 1984)

> As the first full design in the newly renovated Passe Muraille Mainspace, O.D. attempted to fill the large rectangular volume with an environmental feel for both the actor and audience. To achieve this cohesion, the floor of the two storey space was organically raked to unite the two levels and a 40-foot-diameter skycloth was suspended above to complete the envelope. Although focussed on the action of the play, the design intended to give the audience the impression of 'being there.' (JIM PLAXTON)

Plaxton's architectural approach to scenography made him ideally suited to design the renovations of Theatre Passe Muraille's premises on Ryerson Street during the 1983–4 season.[13] Eight years after moving into their permanent premises the company was still using the two stories of the building as separate low-ceilinged theatres. Plaxton's renovations created the 210-seat Mainspace by removing the central section of the upper storey and, leaving the supporting pillars intact, fitting up a balcony around three sides. These renovations exposed the skeletal structure of the building and kept intact some of its idiosyncratic features.

The ground plan for *O.D. on Paradise*[14] shows how Plaxton established a geography for the play. The footprint of the set took up most of the theatre, with the beach, represented by an enormous wedge, rising from the ground floor to the balcony on the opposite wall of the theatre. Most of the spectators were seated along its width. The central section of the stage was taken up with an elongated swirl-like depression reaching down to the water's edge while, upstage, the beach fanned out to a cabana bar, gardens, and a boardwalk into the balcony of the theatre. By stretching the set over the width of theatre in this way, Plaxton presented a cross section of the beach rather than a more conventional perspective that would locate the shoreline either in the audience or upstage as background.

The twenty-seven tons of sand deposited on the massive wooden structure constituted an expansive monochromatic block that squeezed colour out to the margins, and a sky cloth enveloped the spectators in this image of a resort as artificial paradise. The design derived much of its interest for the spectators from the radical spatial allocations combined with naturalistic elements. The spectators were virtually invited to escape into an 'advertisement' for a Carribean resort. Plaxton used black light to endow the actors with an instant tan and he even laid on an island climate in the theatre.

Romeo and Juliet by William Shakespeare (The Dream in High Park, Toronto Free Theatre, 1985, 1986)

The natural hillside amphitheatre in High Park focuses on a grove of very large oak trees. Verona it is not. At 4 times the size of the average opera/ballet stage and without the normal architectural envelope, designing for the park presented unique challenges. Wind, rain and acoustics had to be added to the list of concerns. Two large truck units were the only moving elements in otherwise fixed sets. Walls were designed to reflect sound to the audience much as a megaphone is used. Although the sets were large, the scale was reduced to give the actors a 'larger than life' boost. Extensive use of natural materials and surface treatments were employed both to create the illusion of reality and to tie the sets into the natural environment of the park. (JIM PLAXTON)

Plaxton's designs for outdoor seasons of Toronto Free Theatre in High Park and Skylight Theatre in Earl Bales Park merit special attention. Their integration into the park settings readily identifies them as theatrical counterparts of outdoor installation art.

For *Romeo and Juliet* the upstage façades in both productions were architecturally urban, rather than specifically theatrical – they made no allusion to early modern outdoor stages. In 1985, Plaxton made the downstage area into a two-part village square, complete with a bench in the shade of a big tree. He introduced an important visual dynamic to the set by developing entrances to the downstage area at contrasting angles, and one of the most interesting features was an opening in the arches that defined the square upstage, between the two truck units. The opening was a passageway into an unseen network of small streets in an old city. The staircase in the passageway angled upwards and to stage right and another opening leading in the opposite direction allowed light to flood onto the stairs. This feature – quite unlike a passageway created by Renaissance perspective – relieved the flatness of the façade and accelerated the comings and goings of the actors within a highly charged spatial arrangement of buildings. The spatial compression brought tension into the production.

In the second production of *Romeo and Juliet* Plaxton made further experiments with colour and silhouette and he also re-oriented the downstage area. In 1985 the set was painted to look like aging structures made of brick and covered in stucco; the following year Plaxton changed the palette to grey, matching the buildings and the paving stones painted on the stage floor.[15] The colour change heightened the tragic mood of the production. In 1986 he also changed the geometry of the stage; he rotated the upper portion of the forestage through an angle of 45 degrees so that the steps led towards the upstage right corner and, on the same angle, the corner of a large house intruded into the plaza. The design allowed for a wall with a small balcony on the side of the house, central in the spectator's line of vision, with other architectural structures radiating from it. Other balconies served as crossovers on the face of the upstage wall, enabling onstage connections between various locations. The action could be developed vertically as well as horizontally. Angled like an open book, the 1986 set closed in around the square, making a smaller enclave in the cityscape, even if it was no smaller in actual space. This arrangement also brought acoustic benefits.

Plaxton's design for Skylight Theatre's *Macbeth* in Earl Bales Park, also in 1986, created ruined battlements on a two-part stage. This set, like that for *Romeo and Juliet* in High Park, was enormous, with a footprint of 38 feet × 54 feet and a height of 32 feet.[16] Plaxton designed two platforms of a similar size, at differing heights and defined very differently. The lower one was stage left, closer to the spectators, and resembled a large keystone, with five large slabs, angled upstage away from the spectators, radiating from it and conveying an expansive sense of space.[17] Plaxton arrested the spectator's line of vision at four towers of different heights upstage of the inclined slabs.[18] This lower stage was connected to the upper stage both by ramps and an upstage archway. The upper platform was raised 11 feet above the first and repeated its monolithic structures but, here, two towers at the upstage rim of the platform extended to the height of the surrounding trees. Surrounding this platform was a series of smaller stages behind a parapet, breaking up the volume of the monolith. The two platforms created distinct views, since the lower one showed the full height of an actor's body, while the upper one, with its 'balconies,' presented the actors more cinematically, with only the upper body clearly visible.

Hamlet by William Shakespeare (Phoenix Theatre, 1981)

> Big play, tiny theatre. The only missing element in this traditional design approach to the three-sided thrust is the balcony, which is impossible with a ten-foot ceiling. The circle was used to define and unify the space. The form was repeated as a ceiling ring both to mask the very low lighting grid and create the illusion of more space in the void above. (JIM PLAXTON)

This *Hamlet* was part of the Toronto Theatre Festival of May 1981 and was the final production to be mounted by the Phoenix Theatre in its second-storey premises in a former woodworking shop on Dupont Street.[19] The footprint for this set was 26 feet × 26 feet and it introduced a thrust stage into the 135-seat theatre. Plaxton raised the stage so that it differentiated the performance space from the auditorium. The circular structures above and below were connected with lighting in the ceiling-piece to establish a transparent 'curtain' around the inner square. The strong outer circle and its associated ceiling-piece established the stage space as a round column, contrasted with the squareness of the room itself. Plaxton incorporated existing columns of the theatre structure into his design and added two more to naturalize the architectural support of the ceiling-piece. The strong geometric shapes of this design carried connotations of constructivist scenography, with its nuances of machinery as environment.

In his scenography for other small theatres Plaxton continued to emphasize their intrinsic architectural features. At the Adelaide Court, his design for *The Theatre of Film Noir* by George F. Walker, mounted in the same month as *Hamlet*, 'cracked open' the ceiling with two large ceiling-pieces that were pierced by lights. For the Felix Mirbt puppet version of the Brecht-Weill piece *Happy End* at the Tarragon (1981), Plaxton changed the relationship between stable and movable elements in the set. He created a revolve on the stage that delivered the puppets to the puppeteers and thereby marked the moment when Mirbt's puppets became animated. Also at the Tarragon, for Michael Weller's *Loose Ends* (1980), Plaxton handpainted slides that, when projected from upstage, filled the cyclorama as various vistas of urban desire, ranging from a city park to a neighbourhood backyard, while leaving the stage free for the actors. In creating this production architecture within that of the theatre itself, Plaxton asserted the affinity between scenography and architecture, as distinct from scenography's decorative functions.

Picnic in the Drift by Tanya Mars and Rina Fraticelli (Ice House, Harbourfront, 1981)

> This project was focussed for me on the seductive powers of technology and in particular nuclear technology. The set had to be both large and beautiful. On a tiny budget, material choices were made for 'value' principle – mass produced materials, cheap and available were used to maximum advantage. Fan motors were all surplus, the floor was made of dairy cases (at $2.00 each), the high bridge of paper, all the projection screens were made of vinylon (plastic diaper liner material at 30 cents a yard). Ain't technology grand. (JIM PLAXTON)

Picnic in the Drift was presented in the Ice House, a building formerly used to store blocks of ice, which was being reclaimed by the arts and culture development at Harbourfront.[20] It was a multimedia project by performance artist Tanya Mars and writer Rina Fraticelli; Jim Plaxton's scenography extended the experiment into the use of design materials. Perhaps the most spectacular aspect of this design was the bridge supported by two scaffold towers crossing the expanse of the stage just below the lighting grid, at least twenty feet above the stage floor. Thirty-six feet long and four feet wide, this bridge was made out of sheets of cardboard glued together to a thickness of six inches. It supported not only the weight of a person but also of furniture. The stage floor evoked a high-tech factory which glowed as lighting instruments, inserted under the dairy cases, cast ominous shadows. The arrangement of the playing areas emphasized verticality, but the two video screens with their typed messages and cinematic close-ups of faces presented a strong horizontal axis and a totally different sense of proportion. Also fascinating was the use of the fans, set up on stands like giant flowers on stalks and shifting the air currents when they were turned on. The design presented a surreal image of a garden, with fan-flowers and passing clouds figured on the overhead bridge.

Plaxton had been using cardboard to build sets for several years, delighting in its light weight and strength. For *Strawberry Fields* by Michael Hollingsworth (Factory Theatre, 1973) he obliged the production with an overarching freeway which was flown into position during a blackout.[21] For Sam Sheppard's *Buried Child* (Toronto Free Theatre, 1980) he designed what appeared to be both a realistic two-storey house and a figure for decomposition, with the realistic-looking lath beginning half-way up the wall, as if the plaster had peeled away. In other productions he built upon his earlier experiments and was more daring: for Ibsen's *Lady from the Sea* (Centaur Theatre, 1982) the light weight of cardboard allowed him to create two platforms that were levered up employing a simple wooden scissor mechanism. For *Genuine Fakes* by John Lazarus (Toronto Free Theatre, 1987) Plaxton again primarily employed cardboard, rather than wood, for the construction of a multi-level and complex design.[22]

History of the Village of the Small Huts* and *The Global Village by Michael Hollingsworth (VideoCabaret, Backspace and Mainspace Theatre Passe Muraille, the Theatre Centre, the Studio Café at the Factory Theatre, 1985–98)

The design concept was developed prior to the existence of the History Project as a solution for controlling pin point lighting while eliminating extraneous light, or 'spill.' The black stage box with its tiny openings provided the required masking. *The History* plays provided a perfect fit for the concept, being composed of 20 scenes with an average length of one minute. Lightning quick scene changes could be made simply through shifts in lighting. Actors were never seen making entrances or exits, they appeared out of the void and disappeared. (JIM PLAXTON)

Plaxton's scenographic device of a black box, with precisely focussed lighting from outside the structure, was instrumental in developing a new acting style. The twelve instalments of *History of the Village of the Small Huts* were a fourteen-year project in which Hollingsworth and a committed group of theatre artists retold the history of Canada.

Hollingsworth describes it as 'an epic in progress, a monumental satire on colonialism ... theatre for an audience raised on Rock and TV; history as dramatized by Alfred Jarry, directed by Federico Fellini, performed as a Spike Milligan Goon Show.'[23] Each two-act play, written in a style of popular theatre, is meant as the McLuhanesque 'extended nervous system,' a technological extension of a national consciousness, where images of the Canadian imaginary are realized.[24] Each instalment is populated by about fifty characters performed by about six actors. In order to be ready for their multiple roles performers used white make-up to obliterate their own features and added a wig or a prop to assume the character. Most characterization came through posture, gesture, and facial expression, exploiting idiosyncrasies of the figure being conjured up for the spectators. With about 200 costume changes for each of the installments the pace of each production was frenetic.

Previously, Plaxton's 'machines for acting' had manipulated the time/space relationship by telescoping space and by juxtaposing platforms to create simultaneous locations and effectively eliminate set changes. For *History*, Plaxton reworked these concepts to devise a machine for the performance of history, which enabled Hollingsworth's idiosyncratic montages. While Hollingsworth and costume designers created easily recognizable images of historical figures, Plaxton's scenography was responsible for a structural *découpage* that banished the grounding effect of scenery and put in its place epiphanic moments in history.

The initial design was for the tiny Backspace at Theatre Passe Muraille,[25] but the next instalment had to fit under the balcony of the same theatre's Mainspace. Subsequently, the Theatre Centre and the Factory Theatre Café have been used. All these are very small venues with 100–200 seats. The design of the box has remained relatively stable over the twelve instalments with some adjustment made for the last four of them to accommodate a scrim on which to project a video feed. The first box was constructed totally of cardboard, and all traffic had to flow in one direction across the stage. For later instalments, the box's side walls were replaced by velour curtains, and later yet three passages were constructed on each side, allowing for much more varied movement.

The lighting is completely external to the structure. Openings in the ceiling allow beams of light to be focussed on the stage, as in a pinhole camera. At first, the stage floor was marked below the nine lighting openings so that the actors could either place their *heels* on the mark, so as to place the whole body in the light, or their *toes*, to produce a portrait image. Very soon Plaxton increased the number of openings to twelve and provided side lighting without interfering with the entrances and without narrowing the outer box. For the latest episodes, the side lighting was achieved by means of mirrors affixed to the insides of the box.[26] In the plays of *The Global Village*, television and video conflated the historical events and their encodings. For this effect Plaxton incorporated the above-mentioned scrim as the fourth wall of the box. This impression of a gigantic television screen replaced the imagery based on C.W. Jefferys's 'pictorial reconstructions,'[27] which had been a hallmark of the earlier plays. During the performance, live video feeds of magnified talking heads were projected onto the scrim and, by way of prelude to it, the spectators were presented with a video surveillance of themselves as they took their seats, 'making history.'

Prism, Mirror, Lens by René Highway (Toronto Dance Theatre, Native Canadian Centre, 1989)

> The use of slide projection as a lighting source can give the designer tremendous variety in colour and texture using very few 'instruments.' At the time of this production, I had free access to a computer graphics studio which provided the platform to produce large numbers of required images. 35mm slides were created by shooting directly off a high quality monitor. (JIM PLAXTON)

Beginning in 1985, Plaxton worked in computer graphics for eighteen months, and on his return to the theatre went on to experiment with projections in two important productions. In *Son of Ayash* (Native Earth Productions, 1987) and *Prism, Mirror, Lens* Plaxton explored lighting design which would create a new relationship with the performers – the dancer would enter the beam of the light. In *Prism, Mirror, Lens,* indeed, the source of light was the constant element and the dancer the variable one. Plaxton arranged four projectors on either side of the stage and a ninth above the downstage edge. Each projector was loaded with 80 slides and as the dancers moved, they became screens for the projections. The slides cycled through three main images: a forest, an urban landscape, and finally Norval Morrisseau's *The Bear* simply in outline. Each of these images was repeated in various colours and eventually projected, bleached of colour, as an abstracted shape. By repeating an image in different colours Plaxton investigated the emotional response of the spectators to form and colour. The stunning effect was to eliminate background and foreground in a conceptualization of the spiritual quest of the young aboriginal man of the narrative. This vision of the quest was handled by colour as much as by image and delved into a subjective world of perception, by no means offering to represent an objective forest, or city, or Native symbology. In this case, Plaxton also made the beam imperceptibly horizontal, with no spillage on the floor, so as to create 'live' design – when thought and movement came together.

5

MICHAEL LEVINE

Michael Levine has been a professional stage designer since 1982. Before that he spent a year at the Ontario College of Art and went on to complete a degree in theatre design at the Central School of Art and Design in London. During the 1980s he designed several productions in Britain and was a resident designer for the 1984–5 season at the Citizen's Theatre in Glasgow.[1] During the mid-1980s Levine's work included designs for the Shaw Festival,[2] Tarragon Theatre,[3] and Centre Stage,[4] after which he concentrated on design for opera for a decade. He has designed five productions for the Canadian Opera Company[5] each with a different director, while his work in European and American opera houses has been largely with the Canadian director Robert Carsen, with whom he first collaborated on *Mefistofele* in Geneva and with whom he worked on over a dozen other projects between 1988 and 1998.[6] Between 1988 and 1993 Levine collaborated with Robert Lepage on three productions that were especially notable for their integration of scenography and direction.[7] In 1995 he was the production designer for *September Songs: The Music of Kurt Weill*[8] and since then has worked with François Girard[9] and Atom Egoyan[10] when they have turned from directing film to opera. Recently Levine has returned to non-operatic theatre in Toronto with designs for *Possible Worlds*,[11] *Designated Mourner*[12] (with Julia Fox), and *Platonov*.[13] He has received numerous awards for his work both in Canada and abroad, including a Dora Award for his set and costume design for *Spring Awakening* (1986); the Critics Prize at the Festival D'Aix for Britten's *A Midsummer Night's Dream* (1991); the Scotsman Hamada Prize for both Drama and Music Award at the Edinburgh Festival for *Bluebeard's Castle* and *Erwartung* (1994); and nominations for a Tony and an Olivier Award for Best Design for his collaboration with Voytek on *Strange Interlude* (1986). He represented Canada at the Prague Quadrennial in 1999.[14] He continues to work in Canada, Europe, and the United States.

In Levine's designs for theatre and opera, the visual is continually and actively engaged with verbal and musical expression as the action unfolds. For instance, the pool in *Bluebeard's Castle* appears just in time to receive the pearls that fall into it like tears, and the walls crack to admit in a new order in *Nabucco*. In *Tectonic Plates* large 'cubes' of space served as both geographical and time zones accommodating the dynamics of enactment rather than offering to describe its setting. But Levine's scenography tends also to be conceptual and metaphorical, as with the dresses that became the set in *The Women*, and with the mound of bodies in *Oedipus Rex,* with its inescapable allusion to AIDS. He deliberately varies the scale and proportions of the setting in relation to the performers moving in it. The apprehension of depth is likely to be changed rapidly, giving something of the effect of cinematographic variation, though Levine's manipulation of spatial volumes also gives his scenography a sculptural quality not found in film. And underlying the specific designs, the interactivity of abstract and representational form stands as a continuous reminder of Levine's training as an artist and his familiarity with painting.

The sketchbooks which embody his preliminary and progressively evolved design elements attest to a meticulous attention to detail. Each book is filled with various kinds of sketches – in effect, 'storyboards' exploring how the stage space is to be sculpted, how lighting will be integrated into the design, and often playfully anticipating some challenge or other to the spectators' habits of seeing. A series of sketches may begin as a simple line drawing that evolves several pages later into a watercolour and then into a consideration of the specific materials which will provide texture. In some cases, the sketches work through the lighting as the element under scrutiny, in others Levine concentrates on the colours. At a later stage, Levine moves to maquettes, usually building two. The rougher one uses a 1:50 scale and a second model follows after negotiations and adjustments in the greater detail of 1:25. One of the salient features of these maquettes is Levine's use of them (à la Gordon Craig) to demonstrate precise effects of lighting at crucial moments.

As for his costume designs, these also embody definite ideas about performance. They indicate both the stage setting and attitudes of the wearer in anticipation of their performance context. The social interaction of the characters is as much in evidence as period detail, with groups of characters who can see each other, as it were. This concern with social relationships is particularly characteristic of the costume sketches for operatic choruses. His design process more than justifies Levine's description of himself as 'production designer.'

The Women by Clare Boothe Luce (Shaw Festival Theatre, 1985, Royal Alexandra Theatre, 1987)

> The consumer society. That was in the initial impetus behind the sets and the costumes for *The Women*. The world that Duncan MacIntosh (the director) and I were trying to create was one where there are those who have a lot and must hold onto it. These New York Ladies, the ladies who lunch, are desperately imprisoned by stuff. The tiers of dresses, like wedding cake, reflect, protect and define the world 'The Women' inhabit. We didn't want to have a series of period rooms that would enable the audience to distance themselves from the characters. Through abstraction we attempted to bring the piece closer to the audience of the second half of the twentieth century. (MICHAEL LEVINE)

The design for *The Women* offers a good example of Levine's bold visual narration of the action and his careful consideration of scenographic metaphors. From the preliminary sketches it is evident that Levine focused attention on these women as the measure of all things in Clare Boothe Luce's play.[15] On one double-page spread in his sketchbook he glued nine tiny red tissue paper dresses in a playful hommage to Hollywood costume designer Edith Head.[16] Continuing his inquiry into the connotations of fashion and its revelations of society, he developed these sketches into a grand multi-tiered 'showroom/walk-in closet' consisting solely of red dresses on hangers, towering over a shiny black stage floor. The human scale of the production was maintained by each tier of dresses accommodating a quarter of this *prêt à porter* collection. In the technical drawings Levine reveals his theatrical sensibility. The tiers of dresses were to accommodate about 90 individual garments, each about 6 feet in length, some of them wearable, so that at various time a dress might be temporarily taken from the rack to be used in a scene. The first tier was to hang 7 feet 4 inches from the floor. The red dresses, with their connotations of the special occasions for which they might be appropriate, constantly reiterated the fact of a social arena – the women, at the bridge table, in the dress shop, in the hospital room, in the kitchen, soaking in the bath, or in the beauty parlour, were always to be seen in the context of the quintessentially decisive act of choosing a dress. The colour of the dresses, and thus the set, was unmistakeably the powerful red of the fashion runway and nail polish.

Settings for individual locations were designed to be brought on stage through one of three upstage gaps in the dresses, which remained as a constant visual sign. These portable settings were arranged so as to significantly reorient the sight lines, and even in the individual sets there was always an effort to work against symmetry. The effect was similar to the camera angles in a film that come upon the scene, rather than simply present it head on. Moreover, the details of the design included visual puns – all the chair-backs at the bridge tables had elements of the dresses, bows and sweeps, on them, the scene in the dress shop, by introducing mirrors, heightened the spectators' awareness of women's acute consciousness of being looked at, while the details of the beauty parlour chair echoed the grooming of the hair, hands, and feet of a female body.[17]

The designs for *The Women* sharply define for the prospective spectator the women's socialized behaviour – as both material phenomenon and self-consciousness. Overall, the design shifted the concept of periodization in Luce's play away from objective description of a world to a sense of human power and choice at a moment in time. Ultimately, what is to be evident on the stage is a construction stemming from the women's image-makers – the designers, the beauticians, and the other women – and the self-consciousness that constitutes social and individual perceptions and perspectives. Levine's imaginary extends well beyond costumes into a sensibility figured on the page in, for example, the women's toothy visages, lips outlined in bright red lipstick, hair 'natural bordering on the extremely unnatural,' and carefully manicured red nails.[18] Luce's 'age demanded an image / Of its accelerated grimace,' and Levine was intent on mediating it for the spectators of 1985.[19]

Heartbreak House by George Bernard Shaw (Shaw Festival Theatre, 1985)

There is a license in *Heartbreak House* which allows for a certain freedom to play with the environment. The stage directions outlined by Shaw already deal with a surreal landscape – a room that has been made to look like a ship. We chose to take that metaphor and explore it as far as possible. Christopher Newton (the director) viewed the play as the dream of Ellie Dunn. After entering the house she is led into a seemingly normal 'front room' where she proceeds to fall asleep. While asleep the room grows à la *Alice in Wonderland*. Through this act of transformation we have been liberated from the realistic and we can begin to explore the play from any angle. In the second act we are in the garden of the Estate. It has been transformed to look like the deck of a ship (the topiary that borders the stage has been cut into a wave pattern). We are neither on a ship nor in a garden. A place neither here nor there, very appropriate for the discourse of the play – Pre WWI – a world on the cusp of immense change. (MICHAEL LEVINE)

In *The Women* the tiers of dresses became a kind of vortex filling in the height of the stage; in *Heartbreak House* Levine once again took advantage of the height of the Festival Theatre to animate the walls of the set. In the first act, in which Shaw calls for the highly eccentric but solid setting of a house architecturally mimicking a ship, Levine destabilized the scenic representation. There are suggestions of a reversion to nature in the water damage and the green and red tracings above the doors.[20] An airplane suspended in flight introduced, at the very opening of the play, the threat and excitement of war and destruction with which it ends. By far the most striking element of the set, initially, was the use of books for furniture – knowledge hazardously propping up everything in the Shotover establishment. As the curtain rose, Ellie, just arrived, found herself in an enormous white room with three French doors upstage overlooking a garden, the space impossibly cluttered with piles of oversized books. Then, as she dozed off, the room subtly began to expand. A false ceiling, perhaps 12 feet high when the curtain went up, was slowly raised until the walls and doors soared 30 feet up, so that the contents of the room – including Ellie – shrank alarmingly in relation to their surroundings.[21] In the final scene, which revealed the full depth of the stage, Levine forced the perspective, placing upstage the external façade of the room of the earlier acts and drawing the spectator's eye to it with a line of topiary and the lifelines of Captain Shotover's domestic poop deck. These settings, placing the actors in changing perspectives, made significant comments on the action and blocked a psychological interpretation of it as mere eccentricity.

Mario and the Magician libretto by Rodney Anderson, with music by Harry Somers (Canadian Opera Company, Elgin Theatre, 1992) adapted from the novella by Thomas Mann

The story of the opera is told to us indirectly through the construct of a lecture. We are drawn into the events of the story through the lecturer. Robert Carsen (the director) and I wanted to explore the idea of a memory and ways of visualizing memories. As the lecturer tells his story the onstage listeners are physically taken on that journey. We are transported from winter in Berlin to summer in Italy during the rise of fascism. However, we are not taken to Italy the place, but rather the memory of Italy. We wanted to evoke the quality of a memory rather than the place itself. This could take the form of the way a light hits a face or the movement of the people, how they sit, how they walk. We wanted to create a kind of liquid reality that would allow us to transform from one place to the next seamlessly and have the flexibility of the atmosphere that would enable us to change the mood of the scene in an instant. In the second act we tried to take the audience right inside the memory itself. The auditorium becomes part of the scenery. We as the audience are now part of the transformation from memory into the 'real' world of the opera. As the memory grows stronger we are drawn into it to the point of no return. (MICHAEL LEVINE)

Levine's theatrical sense of space emerges just as clearly in his designs for opera, especially in the way in which he accommodates the chorus. In this production, Levine traced the steps back into memory by using objects to outline simple patterns on the stage. The design elements that Levine emphasized were simple and effective. The pared-down lecture hall remained throughout the lecture in the first act as the reminder of the present, while the straight-back chairs became the mechanism used by the onstage auditors to change the focus to memory, configuring the police station, or turned upside down to signal the beach. The design enabled the chorus to use the elements at hand (coats and chairs to which others were added), a bed arrives, and people cross the stage with suitcases, so that eventually there were enough objects on the stage to tell the story and the chorus could be transformed into the general population of this other period.

As demonstrated in his working models, Levine's scenography sought to confirm the shift that Harry Somers's music and Rodney Anderson's libretto envisioned in their adaptation of Mann's novella. Levine and Carsen presented the cultural oppositions spatially, so that where Stefan had just been speaking, the Police Station took his place. The chairs in the lecture hall had an unremarkable regularity but, when they were moved into the new configuration to suggest an encounter during the vacation in Italy, their neutrality, like that of their occupants, was called into question. When Levine brought suitcases on stage they served to dismantle the regularity of rows in the lecture hall into the definition of a corridor. These effects lengthened or foreshortened the space and presented the chorus either in profile or head on and by doing so in these crucial scenes, Levine obliterated a single focal point. The stage became a space of transience, the length of a corridor between two places. As the model demonstrates, Levine reinforced the shifts in point of view by strong lighting that would direct the attention of the spectator.

In the second act, when the magician was introduced, Levine re-inscribed the notion of the proscenium theatre with conventional sightlines through the Elgin Theatre's proscenium arch, using a stage curtain with the face of the magician emblazoned on it. With the transformation of the stage space complete, the audience was delivered into an illusion that was highly ambivalent – comfortingly theatrical yet, at the same time, perceivable as the alarming aestheticism of the fascist regime. Levine created a remarkable awareness of a voyeuristic stage that frames political power.

Rigoletto by Giuseppe Verdi (The Netherlands Opera, Amsterdam, 1996)

With directors it is always interesting to start from the inside of a piece and work out. I believe it's important to begin with what you are given. In opera you have the role of the chorus which must be taken into consideration. It happens often that there are scenes where you must have up to 70 people on stage and this, of course, has a strong visual impact of its own. To play with this can be exciting.

With *Rigoletto* you are dealing with a society. The structure of that society is the motivating factor onstage. Here we (Monique Wagemaker and Michael Levine) tried to strip the production down to its essential requirements. The sense of place is evoked by the formation of the Chorus. The set played a supporting role in helping to direct the Chorus into different configurations. Essentially the Chorus was trapped by a wall, a physical representation of an imaginary concept – the confinement of society itself. Inside of this wall the players are never allowed to escape. It was essential to have a place without an exit. In the first act there is a low wall on four sides of a square and the chorus are confined within it. In the second act we see a higher version of the same wall. No one is able to leave the confines of the wall. A place where you must die in order to escape. We tried to create a microscope under which we would be able to view the minutiae of that society, as in scientific experiment, we as an audience study the behaviour of Rigoletto. (MICHAEL LEVINE)

Levine's scenography for *Rigoletto* emphasized a hydraulic platform which could be raised 50 centimetres above the floor to serve as a vast dining table for the chorus, or as a stage for Rigoletto, and could also be inclined towards the spectators at either a gentle angle or extreme rake. He used lighting to define the stage space geometrically and not in terms of the shading of perspective. The platform he re-defined throughout the performance: he made it a white or red square in the vast blackness of the stage, he imposed blocks of white and red light on the floor surrounding the platform on all four sides, or he combined the two effects so as to create a red square edged in white. Among the effective uses of the platform was the lighting of just one edge of it, when it was at a steep rake, to create the illusion of a line drawn in space. In a *coup de théâtre* Levine emphasized the surface of the platform when it was brought up to a position almost perpendicular to the stage floor for the final scenes. When Rigoletto mourns over Gilda, her lifeless body lies in the centre of the very white square, as if drawn on piece of paper. By using the platform so intensely and abstracting the space into shape rather than objective context, Levine strongly reinforced the idea of social regimentation and its implacability.

The scenography integrated the chorus so that it often assumed the shape created by the light. In the opening sequence, the chorus was seen lying under red blankets; when they got up and folded them, they placed them around periphery of the platform, prefiguring what would later be created using lighting only. In the second act the chorus was integrated into the red square of light on the platform, and a white light on the top of a wall around them boxed them in. By contrast, in another scene, the chorus was arranged as a red outline around the white of the platform as it became the stage for Rigoletto. Significantly too, the chorus could disappear instantaneously and *en masse* through the 'exits' offered by the platform and the precise lighting design. This interplay of light and choreography allowed Levine to override the architecture of the theatre and constantly reconfigure the stage as an abstract drawing.

Nabucco by Giuseppe Verdi (Bastille Opera, Paris, 1995)

In Nabucco there are two warring factions. The Babylonians and The Hebrews. The world of those who worship idols and those who worship that which does not exist. I wanted to try and play with the friction between these two worlds. Babylonia became a world ruled by gold. The world of the Hebrews was a place of light. Two sides of the same coin, so to speak. Babylonia was a place of endless corridors, a golden prison to perform rituals in. The Hebrews lived in darkness pierced by light. When they are brought to Babylon they bring with them the ability to break open walls, bringing light with them.

The cracks in the walls of Babylon have a double purpose that is interesting on a technical level. I wanted to have large primitive looking spaces, as if made from mud and then covered in gold. It's always necessary to divide scenery in order to transport it. Here we were able to divide the scenery along the crack lines therefore eliminating any straight lines. These fissures became an essential part of the design and helped to underline the fragility of the golden Babylonian world of idols. At the end of the opera Babylon is destroyed, broken to pieces. (MICHAEL LEVINE)

In the production of *Nabucco* at the Bastille Opera[22] in Paris, Levine emphasized the architectonics of the set without an accumulation of plastic elements to denote period or context on stage. Characteristically, Levine had made use of the mobile stages at the Bastille Opera to create a highly metaphorical scenographic structure. As is evident in the maquette, the structure of the set was designed to enforce perspective, and the gold leaf on the walls and ceiling, as well as on part of the floor, reflected light into the centre. In the maquette Levine concentrates on presenting the effect at the end of the opera when the great crack in the structure annihilates the dominant opulent order, and a fresh source of light emanates from what formerly appeared to be solid walls. Levine dismantled the usual continuity of a stage floor to introduce the most spectacular effect in the production from this unexpected angle (rather than above from the flies). He prepared for this moment by making the floor look like dried clay, and at the moment when the fire begins, a flame ran up the crack like lightning and split the stage in two. As the new order is asserted the figures make their way in through the cleft in the clay. This rupture served to show a rent in the pictorial perspective to which the spectators had become accustomed, as the figures emerged from the depth of a core. To complete the image of destruction, Levine brought a wall down in front of the spectators, and when the stage was seen again it 'was covered with gold dust in the air as in the explosion Babylonia has collapsed, and all the people are lying dead' (Levine).

Tectonic Plates by Robert Lepage and Théâtre Repère (du Maurier Theatre, Toronto, 1988; tours to the Cottesloe Theatre at the National Theatre, London; the Tramway, Glasgow)

This was an interesting project that came from Robert's [Lepage] company Théâtre Repère. It began with the original pictures drawn during discussions with Robert, they were comical, reactions, political and direct translations of ideas, it was sketch pad full of ideas. Out of those drawings we began to create a space. In the early stages, the process was Robert's idea and my visual expansion of the actors improvising, working in the design space. What we attempted to do was divide the space without putting up walls, essentially into three blocks, two dry and the pool in the centre, for three different kinds of acting spaces which could all work simultaneously, since Robert was interested in telling simultaneous stories. (There were actually four spaces with the floating [suspended] piano where Chopin played.) We were playing with different time periods and Chopin on a different level also inhabited another time zone.

The design was a direct response to the du Maurier theatre space. In the du Maurier Theatre you could have the audience looking down or alternatively looking up, and that play of looking down at the floor opened endless opportunities for different kinds of acting. These different spatial relationships to the audience worked well with the subject matter.

In the Theatre you are always trying to avoid the uncontrollable; you want to control the environment that you are presenting to the audience. What I find interesting is to introduce an element which you cannot control and which has a life of its own, which feeds the production at another level. So for us, for example it was the water, you can confine it but by its nature the ways in which water responds to people and light qualities are endless. (MICHAEL LEVINE)

Levine's search for an equilibrium of functional and metaphorical space is very evident in his scenography for *Tectonic Plates,* which opened at the du Maurier Theatre at Harbourfront in Toronto, in 1988. This former ice-house has seating in two tiers around the periphery of the performance area and a pull-out section of seats on the main floor. Taking advantage of these fresh sightlines, Levine's design also registers his appreciation of spatial rhythms and Lepage's fascination with props. Levine developed the playing space as three separate sections – an Atlantic Ocean bordered by Europe and North America – so that in itself it narrated the story of the tectonic plates, the movement of peoples from Europe to North America, and a perception across time. Projected onto the floor (including onto the central section occupied by a rectangular pool about one metre deep) was a plan of the tectonic plates as they exist and move under the oceans and the continents. The pool was incorporated into an imagery of mutability that contrasted the connotations of water and land, exhibiting the changeability of the actual and imagined relationships between them. In the constantly changing perspectives of the staging, the pool could both take on the characteristics of the land and possess properties of its own that worked independently of its continental banks, defined by human action: the review of art treasures took the form of images of the great masters projected onto a 'canvas' in the pool; transatlantic crossings were figured when rows of chairs were pushed into the pool; and a new mid-Atlantic culture was presented as an art auction when the chairs were arranged in the pool and the international bidders waded through the water to perch on their backs. 'North America' was identified by skyscrapers made of books with reflective tape glued on for the windows, a bibliomanic architecture that rhymed with the play's characterization of a librarian in New York City, while the music of Chopin emanating from the suspended piano registered another place and time. Overall, Levine's scenography synthesized the multi-dimensional narratives of geography, culture, and space.

In the scenography for *A Midsummer Night's Dream* (1992), another collaboration with Lepage, the two artists experimented further with water as a significant element of the mise en scène. In this case the water and mud became interactive elements in production that the actors exploited. The unpredictable qualities of the water and mud fuelled not only the improvisational process as actors experimented with their effect on movement and sound in rehearsal, but also provided the production with a dynamic edge in each performance in the Olivier Theatre at the National Theatre. For the production of *La Bohème* (1994) at the Vlaamse Opera in Antwerp, Levine experimented with loose sheets of paper on the stage instead of walls and images of a city to define the apartment of Violetta and Rodrigo.

Bluebeard's Castle by Béla Bartók and **Erwartung** by Arnold Schoenberg (Canadian Opera Company, Hummingbird Centre, 1993; tours to New York [B.A.M.], Edinburgh, Geneva, Melbourne, and Hong Kong)

Bluebeard's Castle and *Erwartung* are both about light. In *Bluebeard* we illuminate the dark secrets of Duke Bluebeard's Castle. In *Erwartung* we illuminate the dark secrets of 'The Woman's' mind. We (Robert Lepage and Michael Levine) wanted to have the ability to isolate light and dark, objects in space. The effect that we searched for was being in someone's head. In Bluebeard's Castle there is black gauze downstage of the action held within the structure of the golden frame. The black gauze enabled us isolate light and objects and obliterate what was not essential. In *Erwartung* there is white gauze held within the same frame. The white gauze has the same effect, but it also acted as a projection surface, allowing us to further explore the inner workings of the mind on the surface of the gauze. A golden frame surrounds the action. We wanted to give the pieces some historic context. Both pieces were created at the beginning of the 20th century in the time of Freud and the Viennese school of Egon Schiele and Gustav Klimt. We felt the operas were products of their time, but resonated with our time at the beginning of the 21st century. The frame reflects the obsession of the period with the decorative surface of things and within the frame is the other obsession, that of the interior. (MICHAEL LEVINE)

Michael Levine's scenography for the double bill employed elements of one set for both operas, and the lighting ascribed vastly different metaphorical interpretations to the environments. The gold proscenium framed a set created in forced perspective using two walls and a raked floor. For *Bluebeard's Castle* Levine employed a laser projection of a miniature castle, which revolved slowly in the dark expanse of the stage and introduced the differing scales of representation.[23] He followed through with this altered scale and perspective in the design of Bluebeard's grand hall, where he reduced the seven doorways to seven keyholes – a startling metonymic concentration. The light shining through the keyholes imprinted the shape of the keyhole on the opposite wall producing a disconcerting symmetry. As Judith opened each of the doors an intense beam of light streamed across the stage, dynamically stitching the two sides of the stage together, but also creating a silhouette of Judith framed by the large rectangle of light. The final doorway had the most intense light and ironically made Judith seem much larger because of this brightness. When she opened the door of the greatest sorrows, furthest upstage, Levine amplified the sound of Judith's pearls rolling down the rake as a surreal transmutation of sorrow. The pearls stopped noiselessly as they were absorbed into the river of sorrows, prefiguring Judith's own demise – a descent into the river downstage. In this final image Levine drew attention to the gold frame of the stage as it was lit in red.

For *Erwartung,* Levine focussed the spectator's attention on what had been the neutral and barely visible brick wall opposite the seven keyholes in *Bluebeard's Castle.* His sketches mix the real and the hallucinatory and show how he intended to bring together the imaginary and the real into alignment, an intention that the settings themselves realized. The scenography allowed for a specific orientation for each of the characters, with corresponding entrances and exits to achieve these contrasting angles of perception. Levine cast a light along the wall using the regular rows of brick and mortar to point to the bed and chair of a room in an asylum. Once the setting was established Levine used slides to disrupt the spatial order. He broke the boundaries between the real and the imaginary when the slides not only were distorted but presented a reality which was at a right angle to the stage, so that the wall became a cobblestone street, for example. Thus two perspectives collided in space, using furniture to establish the one and the projections to reinforce the other. Slides projected onto the scrim were used to create a foggy ambiance or showed an impermeable wall encasing the woman in her room. By the fluidity of the images Levine found equivalences for the mimodrama created by the ambiguities of Marie Pappenheim's libretto and Arnold Schoenberg's music.

Eugene Onegin by Pyotr Ilyich Tchaikowsky (Metropolitan Opera, New York, 1997)

The design process of *Eugene Onegin* is an interesting one. The initial design that was presented to the Metropolitan Opera was an extravagant Russian affair with ballrooms and the prerequisite chandeliers. There were technical problems with the design in how it was to fit in the Met's repertoire and in order to accommodate that we felt we would have to alter the essential nature of the design. Robert [Carsen] and I took this as an opportunity to liberate the design from the confines of its realistic setting and allow it to breathe more freely.

We wanted to tell the story from the perspective of Onegin's memory of it. As the curtain rises we see Onegin on stage alone with a letter. The letter written to him by Tatyana. Out of the letter a leaf falls which is then followed by a rain of leaves from above which covers the stage in a thick layer of leaves. The required spaces were then defined by the leaves. Free of scenery we were able to run the story unburdened by heavy scene changes seamlessly moving from one scene to the next. We wanted a space that represented the fluidity of thought and memory.

We transposed the period setting of the piece to the mid 19th century. We felt that the clothes of the mid 19th century, the time of the crinoline and highly decorative dresses, would reflect the bourgeois atmosphere of the story. This was helpful in the last act when we move forward in time to the latter half of the 19th century when clothes for women became more elegant and streamlined reflecting Tatyana's upward mobility in Russian society. (MICHAEL LEVINE)

In his recent opera designs Levine has created fresh relationships between the visual presentation and the music. For *Eugene Onegin* at the Metropolitan Opera in 1997 he had to forego the original sumptuous design, which was a detailed expression of the visual imagination of nineteenth-century Russia the sketchbooks show. When technical exigencies forced a new design, Levine abandoned all the details and opted for a striking simplicity and an impressive monumentality. The final maquette shows the opulent scenery of the earlier design brought down to cut-outs of several birch trees serving as a partial curtain downstage, to denote Madame Larina's estate in the first scene, and instead of a three-dimensional design, Levine designed them so that their shadows, cast on the walls, provided a sense of a garden. The scenography and the production assumed an epic quality and also allowed the music to be played without interruption.

Levine's scenography provided a sense of the space of memory. His design presented the stage as a gigantic box, and the details that he employed struck a telling balance between the human and natural elements. Instead of representing trees, Levine concentrated the design on a flurry of leaves to signal a shift in time. Once they covered the stage floor Levine used them to partition the large Metropolitan stage as they were swept into different configurations so as to outline different spaces on the stage. The walls that rose to the full height of the Metropolitan stage Levine characterized as enormous abstract colour-fields 'painted' by Jean Kalman's lighting design. Suffused in rich tones such as amber or green, the walls provided an ambience that sometimes contrasted with the light which defined the space of the action. Levine focussed on precise details in the costumes. Costume sketches demonstrate how they were researched and conceived with respect to fabrics and trims. Each research page has photos clipped to it and each detail of the costume is numbered. The level of detail in the costumes, within the abstract environment of the set, had the effect of suspending the figures in time, their sensibilities not located in historical particularity.

Dr. Ox's Experiment libretto by Blake Morrison and composed by Gavin Bryars, adapted from the novella by Jules Verne (English National Opera, London, 1998)

In *Dr. Ox's Experiment* there are two distinct worlds. The frozen world of the first act and the melted world of the second act. In Act One we discover a place that has stood still in time and space apart from the modern world, literally frozen in time. It moves at a different pace, a slower pace. An experiment is put upon this place by outsiders. The act of the experiment speeds up this world and defrosts it. We are taken from the medieval world to the present day almost overnight with a fatal effect.

We (Atom Egoyan and Michael Levine) played here with the use of light and gauze. In the first act a black gauze downstage of the action allows us to isolate the light and create a world of candles and light. The white gauze was sewn to the bottom of the black gauze. The white gauze was stored in the floor just below the black gauze and as the experiment is placed on the town, the white gauze rises from its resting place in the floor, it appears as if the 'gas' of the experiment is rising.

Our budget for the production was limited and it was necessary to use as much 'raw material' as available to us in the theatre. In the second act, for example, when the 'gas light' is introduced to the town we lowered the repertory theatre lights to a dangerously low position and supplemented them with more lights on either side. Here we wanted to represent the emotional aspect of the experiment. The danger rather than the physical nature of it. (MICHAEL LEVINE)

For the English National Opera's *Dr. Ox's Experiment*, directed by filmmaker Atom Egoyan, Levine's scenography was keyed to lighting. Initially he defined the space behind the black scrim with general dark blue lighting in which shapes were barely discernible, but as it grew lighter on the stage objects silhouetted against the cyclorama took over the function of defining the place. The pace of life was made evident by the lights on the ends of the slow-moving churn handles and the general darkness was mediated by the candles brought in by the chorus in elaborate holders. As the chorus fanned out on the stage their lights gradually revealed the citizens of Quiquidone. When the citizens hold their town meeting they were arranged on a series of ladders, silhouetted against the cyclorama, so that the human figures were perceived predominantly as two-dimensional until the arrival of the energy which added the shading of third dimension. As for Dr Ox and his assistant Ygène, who observe the village from a flying machine, Levine devised a secondary stage – using the proscenium arch and the scrim. He located the balloon in which they were flying along the top of the arch, and presented the village as miniature houses on the stage floor. The expanse between the two was handled by lighting on the scrim which obscured the stage behind it. Levine's scenography thus created layers in the depth of the stage – the first was a territory occupied by Dr Ox with his specialized, highly portable scientific paraphernalia, the second was for the citizens, and the third presented the technology, churns, of Quiquidone. He contrasted the dark depths of the stage with a near two-dimensionality for Ox and Ygène when he set them vertically on the 'surface' of the scrim.

To show that the gas was being infused into the community Levine used a white scrim attached to the base of the black one that had reinforced the sense of darkness on stage. As the scrim rose it imparted the sense of a mist rising and the spectators became very conscious of the stage as a large cube. The effects of electricity were evident in changes to individual elements on the stage – the churns no longer had lights on their handles, but wires connected them to an invisible source, and Levine defined the edges of the stage more clearly by a secondary proscenium arch created by lowering the lighting instruments to outline the space. For the final melting of the crystalline environment, Levine replaced the borderless darkness of the first scenes with portable lighting booms to create a cube defined by lights. On each side of the stage Rick Fisher's lighting design used ten booms that held hundreds of lamps, while just as many created the luminous ceiling that displaced the sky. To signal the melted snow Levine used the white scrim as a gigantic screen on which the reflections of patterns on the surface of the water in the puddles on the stage could be seen. Levine's scenography realized both a scientific voyeurism of the new Quiquidone but he also created a theatricality that was rooted purely in the technology of the theatre – where wires and water were 'too' close for comfort, signalling a new self-reflexive presence of the scenography. Moreover, where in the first scenes the chorus carried in the points of light on stage, by the final sequence the technology of the theatre takes over the role of the chorus.

6

KEN MACDONALD

Ken MacDonald trained as a painter and a teacher at the University of British Columbia and from 1972 to 1977 taught art in a Vancouver high school. He ventured into professional theatre when he helped a friend[1] with some artwork for a production. This project led to his designs for the inaugural season at the Belfry Theatre in 1977,[2] after which he turned increasingly to scenography. He has designed productions for large theatres such as the Vancouver Playhouse as well as for smaller houses, such as the (now demolished) Seymour Street Theatre in Vancouver and the Tarragon in Toronto. Among the various companies he has worked with are Touchstone, Tamahnous, Green Thumb Theatres, Studio 58 at Langara College, and White Rock Summer Theatre.[3] MacDonald has also designed operas for the Banff Centre for the Arts[4] and for the Vancouver Opera Association,[5] and was the art director for two music videos.[6] The selection of designs included below demonstrates his scenographic engagement with a range of theatre technologies and spaces from low-ceilinged, shallow stages to large houses with fly towers. Characteristically, his stage compositions create strong metaphors to narrate the action and demand intellectual engagement with the scenographic aspects of the performance. MacDonald is the winner of thirteen Jessie Richardson Awards in Vancouver[7] and three Dora Mavor Moore Awards in Toronto. His design for *The Overcoat* was part of the Canadian exhibit to the Prague Quadrennial in 1999.

MacDonald has collaborated regularly with playwright, actor, and director Morris Panych. Between 1982 and 1988 they created five political cabarets for which MacDonald was the composer, musician, and performer.[8] This artistic relationship has continued chiefly as one of playwright with scenographer. MacDonald has designed the premiere productions of all of Panych's plays[9] and, significantly, elements from his designs have been used for the covers of the published texts, to which they are integral. In the introduction to his triptych of plays for young audiences, Panych emphasized the centrality of the visual presentation of his plays and for this reason included MacDonald's accounts of the scenography.[10] The idiosyncratic spaces that MacDonald has designed to enable Panych's storytelling have engendered a surrealistic style of performance and narration.

On occasion Panych and MacDonald have collaborated as director and scenographer of works by other authors, such as Carlisle Floyd's opera *Susannah* (1997), *The Company* (1995), and *The Overcoat* (1997). The latter two were wordless performances which – largely through the scenography – maintained a dramatic focus rather than becoming narrative dance. And MacDonald's elaborate and glittering stage machinery was entirely congruent with H.G. Wells's writing in the participatory entertainment *The History of Things to Come* (1999)[11] as it whisked volunteers from the audience away into another dimension.

As he goes to work, MacDonald often starts a design by folding a piece of paper into the shape of a potential set and lighting it with an architectural lamp to look for the interesting shadows. He works out the total effect to be achieved in small sketches and models where he can investigate the palette, the intensity of colour, or the sense of proportion between the design elements. He concentrates on the juxtaposition of elements rather than representation to arrive at his scenography. MacDonald's designs develop visual rhythms that the actors complete as they move through the space, since his scenography is very much part of the temporal-narrative structure of the performance. Take, for example, the oversize elevator arrow-gauge in *Lawrence and Holloman* (1998) that remains unchanged on stage, pointing to a stopped time, and, seen within a setting of an enormous blue skyscape with clouds, seems to have been liberated from the building, declaring a new kind of space-time relationship. Into this combination inner-outer environment settings that suggest location are brought onstage to focus individual scenes.

MacDonald likes to infuse the stage with trompe l'oeil effects, radically manipulating perspective, composition, and colour so that spectators observe the components of the scenography before they discern the overall metaphor being developed. To this end MacDonald prefers to work in theatres with a proscenium arch, which acknowledge illusion-making and give him more complete control over the spectators' point of view. His denial of perspective and his forced perspectives strongly affect the overall style of the performance, including the acting. In theatres where there is no proscenium arch he often invokes a strong geometry in the sightlines, creating zones of intensity by shape or colour. His scenography for Judith Thompson's *White Biting Dog* in Toronto (1994) actively complicates perception by using multiples of clearly defined spaces. MacDonald's own photographs of his designs have been chosen for this study since they provide a distinct view of the complexity of his work and the craftsmanship they require, in the realization of which he is very much involved.

The Imaginary Invalid by Molière (Arts Club, Granville Theatre, 1996); **The Game of Love and Chance** by Pierre Marivaux (Arts Club, Granville Theatre, 1996); **Waiting for the Parade** by John Murrell (Vancouver Playhouse, 1995)

In the design for *The Imaginary Invalid* I played with the sense of a farce and pushed everything in the design to the ridiculous: I started with the idea of three doors to play farce and I multiplied the number of doors to nine; I used a forced perspective for the ante-room in which the action takes place. This set created an impression of a once beautiful and opulent home and showed a faded glory and decrepitude with its Dufy-ish water-stained wallpaper. Other details I made very graphic – the chair on which Orgon sat was a toilet/ chamber pot/throne, with contents that the doctors examined and an almost excessive number of medical instruments were exaggerated by their baroque-like quality. The set became a visual gag once the actors appeared. The door heights ranged from 9'11" down-stage diminishing to 2' upstage, and the chair placed in the apex was perspectively proportionate at 1' tall. We (Morris Panych and Ken MacDonald) continued the ridiculous into the performance. We made the actors enter through the downstage doors, but upstage where this was impossible, they propelled only a part of their body onto the stage, and would literally peer over the upstage wall to overhear conversations and observe the action.

For *The Game of Love and Chance*, I used similar elements with deliberate rhyming with *The Imaginary Invalid*, but this time I used the metaphor of a nautilus and concentrated on curves rather than angles. These doors also diminished in size, but this time they were arrayed across the stage. We set the production in 1956 and I wanted the design to show that the house in which the action was taking place was not of the same period as the action, that it was not a brand new house – so this mansion was a glorious 1920s art deco home in contrast to the *haute couture* costumes inspired by Dior and Chanel of the mid-1950s. These two strong impressions of style and fashion worked on the stage to make the differences between the place and the people very visual.

Rather than using walls to create perspective for *Waiting for the Parade*, I created the illusion of the expanse of the prairies as a distinct space for the action. The main platform was constructed out of planks that were very carefully cut to fan out from a vortex at the vanishing point on the horizon. The station house (on a separate platform on the stage right side of the stage) was built to scale so that it was 5' high at its downstage edge but was only 1' in height upstage. The sky was also painted in perspective, as I played with emphasizing a vanishing point on stage. The actors could maintain the illusion as long as they stayed downstage of the station house and closer to the musician's piano on a separate platform to stage left. At the intermission we had to keep the audience members from getting up on stage to test the proportions of the station house. (KEN MACDONALD)

Looking at the designs, one might suppose that MacDonald has applied to the stage the rules of perspective in painting. The rake and geometrical scaling of objects to establish proximity in relation to the vanishing point seems at first to characterize the stage as a two-dimensional canvas. In fact, *The Imaginary Invalid* and *The Game of Love and Chance* employed an exaggerated or hyper-perspectivalism as a visual enhancement of authorial plotting and humour. For *The Imaginary Invalid* MacDonald introduced a few exemplary architectural details to reinforce the proportions. The junction of two ceiling cornices, along with the rake, created a vanishing point about a third of the way up the upstage wall and the nine doors, distributed asymmetrically on the two walls, diminished in height so as to establish a long hallway in a large house. The initial impression of depth was reinforced by the large free-flowing floral wall decoration, as well as three-dimensionally by the upstage chair. The set reinforced Molière's themes of social power and served to create the spectacle of Orgon – an overblown ego, out of proportion with everything around him. The incongruity of the human with the scenic proportions, marked particularly by the entrances of the actors, became an important thematic device. Orgon, played downstage, was part of a naturalistic action of which the schemers became surrealistic voyeurs as they peered at their handiwork over the top of the wall.[12] MacDonald's metatheatrical scenography doubled the pleasure of seeing.

When he used a forced perspective for the production of *The Game of Love and Chance* MacDonald reiterated an architectural setting already familiar to those who had seen the previous season's production of *The Imaginary Invalid*. He rotated the earlier design through ninety degrees, did without the second wall and the eye-guiding cornice and instead made the wall descend into the vanishing point. By presenting the perspective as if in profile, he suggested an actual vanishing point perpendicular to the front of the stage, which thus figured a vortex. The spectator was prodded into shifting the stage back to a head-on view, returning to a geometric perspective, as it were. The ingenious effect was to bend the spectator's vision around the imaginary corner. For this production MacDonald made the top of the wall a ramp cross the line of vision just at the point where the spectators would expect the vanishing point. And instead of the minimal set pieces of the earlier experiment, he introduced spherical lights and rounded furniture that echoed the final curve of the ramp. The bright red of these design elements, against the purple and green of the vegetation painted on the walls, created eddies of energy punctuating the width of the stage and disrupting the perspectival effect. Using the ramp as an idiosyncratic entrance, actors could descend into the very vortex, or be 'absorbed' into the roundness of the furniture. This scenography once again posed a challenge to traditional use of doorways as the architecture of comedy by employing complementary lines of vision, which implicitly denied a single-perspective vantage point. In contrast to the art deco of the set, MacDonald's costumes alluded to Chanel and Dior, the high fashion of mid-twentieth century, and this juxtaposition of the two periods set up an energetic conflict between their dynamism and also between timeless characterization and traditional theatrical milieu.

In the design for *Waiting for the Parade*, MacDonald abstracted a prairie landscape that 'naturally' provides a sense of distance. His scenography focussed on a station platform and was in keeping, visually and metaphorically, with the suspension of time in Murrell's sequence of departures and arrivals, farewells and greetings, memories and hopes. The station building in the panoramic sweep of a landscape, silhouetted against the sky, replaced the multiple locations of Murrell's mise en scène and was both a function of memory and a projection into the future. MacDonald balanced the bulk of the station house by installing a piano on a similar wing off the main platform on the stage left side, coupling visual effect and music. Maintenance of perspective limited the actors' movements to the area downstage of the two platforms and, in so doing, effectively configured a temporal split in spatial terms. *Here* was *now*, and *there* was *before* or *after*. In this design there was no cross-over element (such as the chair in *The Imaginary Invalid*) that would disturb the gravity in this instance of the visual genre. The somewhat circumscribed acting area intensified the emotional import of the action by bringing it close to the audience and leaving specific physical contexts ambiguous.

7 Stories by Morris Panych (The Arts Club, Seymour Street, 1989); ***Death and the Maiden***
by Ariel Dorfman (Vancouver Playhouse, 1993)

For the first production of *7 Stories* at the Seymour Street Theatre the stage was very shallow so I used its height. It was a way of creating a space that could be surreal, an idea that comes from the paintings of René Magritte. As a designer one of my fascinations is with skies as an important part of the design. In *7 Stories* the sky became the structure for the set, much as the glass walls of many contemporary buildings reflect the world around them, but themselves disappear. I also wanted to play with reversed perspective of the building so that the audience experienced the Man's point of view from the ledge.

For the production of *Death and the Maiden* I began by creating the sky as a collage – as if it had been assembled from torn fragments of a painting and the ragged edges of the tears could clearly be seen against the cyclorama. The clouds and the moon were cut-outs mounted on thin plywood for a three-dimensional effect. The moon became linked to the interior of the beach house since it was framed between two columns of full length sheer curtains. Because the sky was three-dimensional we could change the moon from its full roundness to a small crescent to coincide with the discoveries in the action. The turbulence of the monochromatic blues and greys behind the stylish grey wrought iron gates downstage made the beach house an uneasy retreat. (KEN MACDONALD)

The scenography for *7 Stories* is a notable example of MacDonald's transformation of spatial perception in his scenography. His design was based in the moment of simultaneity – when the mirrored glass on a building paradoxically cedes its mass to the streetscape that it reflects, denying itself in the expression of the very qualities that constitute it. Similarly, MacDonald's scenography zeroed in on the act of spectating in the theatre – the voyeurism of the fourth wall. The flat upright 'wall,' into which seven shuttered windows had been cut above a small ledge about 18 inches wide, was a physical barrier that denied pictorial perspective on this stage. Emphasizing the surface and creating glimpses of depth in the small compartments, MacDonald suggested the evanescence and lightness of existence. The clouds on the window-shutters were painted in a counterrhythm to the façade, producing the intriguing illusion of something like a rearview mirror that was disturbed by the entrance of the performers. Moreover, this use of stage painting redefined the basic conventions of a performance space. Here, the main part of the stage was the site of emptiness and, indeed, extinction, while the severely restricted playing space of the ledge further emphasized the spaciousness of the rooms behind the shutters into which the spectators could peer but without finding any defining characteristics.

The design for *Death and the Maiden* on the large stage of the Playhouse combined the concept of a domestic environment with that of the monumentality of the Greek tragic stage. MacDonald's painted collage of a sky used the same monochromatic palette of blues and greys with magenta accents that was used for furniture, and the dialogue between the two was accentuated by setting the clouds at a steep angle to the floor. The turbulence of the sky was reiterated by different means – by the stylized grey wrought iron gates located downstage that contrasted with the linearity of the furniture. The 18-foot blue wooden table and its six spindle and press-back chairs were menacingly grand as the sole furniture in the 47-foot width of the proscenium opening. Architectural elaboration was transposed into the folds of the sheer curtains that when pulled to the sides appeared as gigantic white columns. Progressively during the performance attention was focussed upstage on the moon, which ultimately became an almost exclusive object of contemplation as the curtains served to create a false proscenium arch framing it.

White Biting Dog by Judith Thompson (Tarragon Theatre, 1994)

One of the original ideas for the design that the director Morris Panych and I considered was to have a big couch drop from the flies and land in the middle of the stage. Eventually we decided to do away with any furniture on the stage and considered the stage part of a big science experiment conducted by the father, as if the house were turning back into nature. The set was painted to look like a mossy forest, complete with increased moss growth on the North side, and trees were growing in the walls with their branches reaching into the rooms. Natural decay and the luminescence of decaying wood was replicated on the stage by making the light emanate from within the walls through the exposed lath, and from the floor between the boards. We extended the idea of the father's fixation with peat moss by jars of rotting organic material that lined the walls as if taking it over.[13] They provided the central structure to the set as the idea of the father stuffing bits of organic material into the house literally became part of the design. We never did add furniture to the set, but actors could sit on the stairs. (KEN MACDONALD)

The longer the spectator observed it the stranger the house became. Completely plausible lath and plaster walls became luminescent, windows looked out on incomplete walls, and the very structure of the house, with trees flourishing in its walls, was ceded to the natural world. MacDonald concentrated the attention of the spectators by employing a series of geometric forms that stood in for the absent proscenium. The shelves of moss preserved in Mason jars outlined passageways and walls. Paul Mathiesen's lighting allowed wisps of light to penetrate through the cracks where the forest was intruding, and set this house adrift from reality. The lath-work of the walls became shutters through which miniature vistas emerged, and the whole house floated up on the light coming through the floor. The spectators were presented with a scenographical enactment of the processes of decay and a transforming, surreal luminosity of vegetativeness.

The Overcoat conceived and directed by Morris Panych and Wendy Gorling (Vancouver Playhouse, 1997), based on the novella by George Gogol to music by Dimitri Shostakovich[14]

The image of a factory with its banks of windows dominated the initial development; I was influenced by a black and white photo of an old factory or warehouse in Milwaukee and some real buildings such as the B.C. Rogers Refinery in Vancouver. I created a wall of windows upstage that could be lit from the front and behind and could have multiple openings, so that it could be seen as different places. *The Overcoat* was totally set to music and the need was for all the things on stage to work choreographically and maintain the momentum of the action. All the furniture on the set was on casters so that it could be partnered with the actors; the stairs, depending on how they were brought on stage, could signal three very different locations. While thinking of the design I saw a tailor's old treadle sewing machine in a store window near my home and bought it, because I knew that we would need at least one sewing machine. As I began to draw the machinery I started to abstract the components and colours from it so that these very small parts of a machine became the large wheel and the gears. (KEN MACDONALD)

Structurally, the scenography for *The Overcoat*, like that for *Ends of the Earth*[15] and *The Company*,[16] recalls MacDonald's earlier career as a musician and composer. In the earlier productions MacDonald had integrated a counter rhythm to the human movement by employing a conveyor belt. For *Ends of the Earth* the belt, conveying performers, was at the base of the upstage wall as part of a vision of cogs, wheels, and steps. This area became a zone of transformation. In *The Company* MacDonald created a figurative mechanization that was partially visual with identical cubicles, each with a naked light bulb, and each with a tiny grimy window, which was reiterated by means of backlighting as an even smaller rectangle on the stage floor. The regularized grid of the compartment eliminated a vanishing point and implied that the choral movement on the stage was the multiplication of a single figure. For this production MacDonald moved the conveyor belt onto the stage so that it became a physical link between the upstage and downstage areas, a means of transport angled so as to convey also a skewed perspective.

In *The Overcoat* MacDonald revisited the repetitive pattern for the upstage area that he had used in *The Company*, but instead of a conveyor belt MacDonald set all the furniture on casters and the doors of the upstage wall on silent rollers. The upstage wall afforded some dramatic effects as MacDonald resisted the solidity of his other designs in the conception of this translucent structure. Alan Brodie's lighting design identified the wall as either an interior or exterior space by the direction of the light, but when individual doors were raised the reality of architecture was ceded to the wall as a choral space. Open doors gave forth onto colour-saturated 'compartments' that served to re-orient the stage instantly to a verticality and afforded a distinct choral presence, one that was in a different spatio-temporal relation to the main action, akin to a cinematic still in the flow of the choreography. The wrought iron staircase could be wheeled into position to suggest different buildings, and other scenic elements were swiftly and smoothly introduced by means of the fly tower machinery. Timing the arrival of the elements of the set was a job for director as conductor who had to harmonize the choreography of performers and scenography. The activity of the drafting office modulated into an elaborate dance in which the drafting tables became the obliging dance-partners of the clerks. By contrast MacDonald presented the tailoring sweatshop as a two-part machine: on stage right a large wheel descended from the flies and took all the strength of two peons to power it, while on stage left the lighting revealed, one by one, a chorus of undifferentiated tailors not so much operating their machines as being absorbed into them by their job. MacDonald thereby extended the concept of a chorus to the 'things' on stage and these two scenes provided incisive visual commentaries of the inhuman industrial order by integrating all labourers into the machines of their trade. MacDonald also created a few purely representational elements, such as the gold-nibbed pens, but these were in a totally different scale. The imposing

22-foot height of the pens made them into quasi-architectural features just as the wheels of imaginary equipment dwarfed their operators. The lines on the stage floor were both receptive of the choreography and suggestive of architectural drawings. Throughout, the scenography juxtaposed the images of highly efficient and inhuman industrial order – albeit images frankly produced by contemporary stage technology – and the Chaplinesque figures inhabiting it.

2000 by Joan McLeod (Tarragon Theatre, 1996; Vancouver Playhouse, 1997)

The challenge and unique opportunity for me working on these two productions of *2000* was that they were designed back to back with very different directors and in very different spaces. I always search for the big metaphor so that the stage becomes another landscape that fills the space. At the Tarragon the forest where the Mountain Man made his home was a terrarium in the centre of the stage, that also served as an inner courtyard of an urban house. It was a totally different environment. The forest was very real – real bark and moss glued onto wire forms. The Man was dressed in a brown suit with moss growing on the 'north side' of him so that he was hardly differentiated from his surroundings. In the kitchen the high tech designer appliances were everywhere but nature was present as the painting of leaves directly on the walls and as the images of animals in the light box artworks.

For the Vancouver production the director Patrick MacDonald wanted the location on stage to look very West Coast. I combined the concept of abstract images as in paintings by Lawren Harris with the clarity and simplicity of Japanese design by using geometric shapes and dividing the stage space architecturally into two levels. The conical evergreen tree, upstage centre remained on stage throughout the performance. When defined by a red picture frame it signalled an interior and when surrounded by large sono-tube trees became part of the forest. Interior locations were dominated by a pronounced angularity and distinct textures, the slate floor and shiny black leather couch, contrasted the rounded rocks and trees of the forest. (KEN MACDONALD)

The difference between the Toronto and Vancouver designs for *2000* resided in the distribution of details through the scenographic elements. In Toronto the terrarium – using real moss, rocks, and bark – created a West-Coast chic as it captured the wilderness in the courtyard/centre of the home. The forest was central in the visual rhythm of the stage, but the actual lushness of the forest was an insert, in the glass box. The relative closeness of the spectators in the smaller theatre allowed for a surrealistic effect – the cube in the centre of the stage was at once a prominent architectural feature, defining an elegant urban courtyard, and a boundary for the Mountain Man, and yet it appeared to be more real than the high-tech environment that surrounded it. Other elements of the forest were distributed on the set as artistic renderings of wilderness, such as the image of the cougar in a light-box panel painting (by lighting designer Paul Mathiesen) in the kitchen and the murals in turquoise and green of natural features. MacDonald's almost scientific observation of nature in this set made the centre of the stage a clearly defined, visually intrusive, and anomalous zone. While the actors had to work around it, the spectators could see through it and enjoy the lively perspective of the Grandmother. The transparency of the cube also lent itself to varied and significant lighting effects whereby, for example, the encroachment of the forest could be marked as shadows cast by the trees on the floor of the house, or the yellowness of the Grandmother's bedroom on one side of the cube imparted an interior light to it. The shadows of the branches were the negative counterpart of the painted white tendrils and leaves on the upstage wall. Since the scenographic palette included painted images, light and natural elements were particularly emphatic. The oranges in the wire basket precisely placed on the kitchen counter were rather more compositional than edible but also introduced an image of perishability in the high-tech design of the kitchen.

For the production at the Vancouver Playhouse MacDonald shifted the relationship between the forest and the house, so that the high-tech design abstracted the depiction of the West Coast forest in a totally different manner. He introduced mechanisms to confuse the locational categories, superimposing one on the other. Lawren Harris–inspired contrasts in abstract shapes and textures displaced the vegetative of the forest in the painted backdrop, and the fly tower allowed MacDonald to re-use elements rather than juxtapose them. The various elements worked in two environments depending on how they were presented: the conical tree, echoing Harris, functioned ambivalently as a real vista (when contained by the red frame) and as a self-declared painting. This frame, like other elements – the blue tubes standing in for trees, the carved rocks, and the stylized totem pole – was flown into place, enabling quick and economical redefinition of the upper level, which figured an aestheticized natural landscape. About thirty inches below this was the dining room. With the table the height of the upper stage, its slate top blended in shape and colour with the tiled floor of the upper level, but the surrounding bench seating also made it into a miniature Japanese stage with *hanamichi*. MacDonald re-characterized the space upstage as a Zen garden by his insistence on shape and colour rather than function. Moreover, seen from the perspective of the spectator, the appeal of the lines of the leather couch in front of the red blinds of the window, or the high-tech kitchen, was as approximations of the simplicity of Japanese design. There was an acute poignancy in the gradual realization that the Grandmother, dependent on a walker, could not get to the dining room, which MacDonald had characterized as purely aesthetic. Her belief in the Mountain Man kept her on the slate grid of the upper level, closer to the forest.

Hamlet by William Shakespeare (Arts Club, Stanley Theatre, 1998); **Anatol** by Arthur Schnitzler (Belfry Theatre, 1993); **The Necessary Steps** by Morris Panych (Arts Club, Seymour Street, 1991)

The red, white and blue used in *Hamlet* were taken from the contemporary Danish and Norwegian flags and then made into three-dimensional abstract compositions. I took advantage of the fly tower in the theatre to create large areas of intense colour, reminiscent of Mark Rothko's large colour fields. By intensely colouring these backdrops with the lighting, the 55-foot wide expanse and 25-foot height assumed a powerful Japanese-like look. Throughout the performance I maintained the starkness and cleanliness in the design by using very few elements on stage: 5 black benches that the actors moved into position, while the blue poles and white and black arrases were flown in. The effect was to create a stark sense of location through minimalism. During the curtain call the intense redness, blueness, and whiteness of the drops was dispersed as they were raised in succession to reveal the black back wall of the theatre with several real ladders leaning against it.

The repetition of a simple element can be very effective on stage and this was the case with the drawers for Anatol. Using the Arc de Triomphe as the structure for the architecture, this wall of drawers provided storage for all the necessary props and retained a certain unpredictability on stage throughout the performance. Some of the drawers could slide open individually, as if they were part of an enormous filing cabinet, while others were simply the façade for larger storage spaces. Each of the seven scenes started with access to the drawers and for some of them drawers were removed from the wall to become the furniture, for others, the wall was used as a projection screen and the images overwhelmed the individual details that the spectators had become so familiar with.

The Necessary Steps is a play about a man who exchanges his shoes with a tramp. These 'magic' shoes 'careened' him to unexpected places on an incredible journey. He could go anywhere as the slides projected on the Escher steps spirited him immediately to a new place. The recognizable location – a forest, a wheatfield, a city-scape, or night sky – would flash on the wall and then slowly fade out as the lights came up on the scene. (KEN MACDONALD)

The venue for Hamlet was the new space of the Arts Club, the 650-seat Stanley Theatre. MacDonald's minimalist design was adapted to the wide, shallow stage, drawing on a contemporary Japanese aesthetic. A primary effect of the design was to contrast the horizontal and vertical axes of the stage without reference to perspective. The scenography was kept simple, though it made extensive use of the 37 fly lines to bring down such items as the black or the white arras, by means of which MacDonald could significantly re-orient the stage and change its visual atmosphere. The actors, on stage throughout the performance, had active scenographic 'roles,' moving the black benches into new configurations to suggest hallways or passageways, and also made a more purely visual contribution by their distribution on stage. The upstage expanse of the cyclorama was lit by vibrant reds or cool blues to draw out the brush strokes and impart texture. Along with the pure strains of colour in the individual elements this scenography created a landscape in which the import of a scene was carried partly by the colours.

The intensity of abstract art used in Hamlet was also evident in earlier designs, such as those for Anatol and The Necessary Steps, productions that took place in theatres of different sizes. The enormous chest of drawers for Anatol functioned in concert with the slide projections. Together they enacted a totally different sense of place and scale – the storage capacity of the drawers constantly divided up the space, while the projection of the body onto them was at least double the height of the actors. Thus the stage was transformed into a repository of images and tableaux. By contrast, the reference to M.C. Escher's drawings[17] for The Necessary Steps denied the spectator a single point of view. Shading created plausible steps on the upstage wall that would defy gravity. Images projected onto the wall had the effect of a photographic 'afterburn' that occurs after the flash has gone off. The spectators encountered the perceptual riddle of which steps would ultimately work, and were entertained with the possibility of an inversion of the whole stage image.

7

TERESA PRZYBYLSKI

Teresa Przybylski completed her training in design in Poland with an MA in architecture at the Technical University in Cracow and an MA in fine arts, with specialization in film, television and theatre design from the Academy of Fine Arts in Cracow, and had worked as an architect and a designer in Poland and West Germany before coming to Canada. She opened her design studio in Toronto in 1988. A decade later she had created nearly a hundred designs for theatre, opera, and dance companies in Toronto, Ottawa, Peterborough, Stratford, and the United States, and had been awarded two Dora Mavor Moore Awards. Her designs for *Marcel Pursued by the Hounds*[1] were part of the exhibit of the Associated Designers of Canada in the Prague Quadrennial in 1999. She has worked extensively with the mime companies Theatre Smith-Gilmour[2] and Theatre Columbus in Toronto. She has also designed productions for Native Earth Performing Arts, Necessary Angel, Nightwood Theatre,[3] Young People's Theatre,[4] Tarragon Theatre, Buddies in Bad Times Theatre, Mixed Company, Theatre Volcano, Theatre Orangeville, Danny Grossman Dance Company, Théâtre Français de Toronto, Pleiades Theatre, VideoCabaret, Theatre Passe Muraille, the Stratford Festival,[5] Pacific Opera, the Canadian Opera Company,[6] Opera Theatre of St Louis, the Atlantic Theatre Festival, Odyssey Theatre in Ottawa, and Arbour Theatre in Peterborough.[7] Most of the companies for which she has designed use rented space in post-industrial buildings, all of which make their own distinctive demands on the scenographic imagination.

As one might expect of a designer trained in Poland, Przybylski prefers the term scenography to describe her work, since it connotes the comprehensiveness of the process that brings together the existing architecture with concepts of the particular production. Characteristically she takes images associated with the sun and the elements of water and earth as the triadic basis of her scenography. Water's fluidity develops a consciousness of the movement on stage, which will bear on the choice of the materials that will be used to develop the visual rhythms. Earth enters into the design process as the plasticity of the shapes on the stage and how they take up space. Przybylski is always concerned with conceptual exploration of the plays and, in this respect, finds the relationship between the first two elements and the third member of the triad very important. This third member, the sun, enables the interplay of light and shadow, the contribution that the lighting of the given elements makes to the production.

One of Przybylski's first designs in Toronto was for Büchner's *Woyzeck* (1988) for the Canadian Stage Company in the downstairs theatre at Berkeley Street. Remarkable in this scenography was the verticality of her design for a production that used puppets created by Felix Mirbt. She incorporated hydraulic elevators on either side of the stage to carry the two female narrators to the reading stations. The proportions and technology might have overwhelmed the four-foot-high puppets and their human manipulators on the stage floor. They did not do so, since the elevators extended the metaphor of mechanization from the puppets to the narrators who were transported into their location. Moreover, the elevators provided a structure to the space by excluding the side space on the stage by creating the vertical focus. This spatial configuration, separating the vocal expression from the physical action, made explicit Büchner's distinction between the personal experience and the social structures that allow people to treat their fellow citizens so ill.

When Teresa Przybylski was the resident designer at Young People's Theatre her scenography had to take advantage of the proportions of a building which had once been an engine shop. Her design (set and props) for *Whale* by David Holman filled the great expanse of the stage – 60 feet wide, 21 feet deep, and rising more than 20 feet to the lighting grid. The setting was the Arctic. Employing heavy fire retardant paper in wide strips layered like the ice-blocks of an igloo, Przybylski created the craggy, icy landscape of the Inuit and the underwater habitat of the whales. Human and cetaceous denizens cohabited in the one set without changes to it. Lighting by Steven Hawkins was fundamental to the layering of the elements of the set and also indicated where the action was taking place: a cool white emphasized the harshness of the landscape, casting shadows on the paper blocks to suggest drifts and icy crags, while bluish lighting that suffused the stage exploited the translucence of the paper to figure the underwater icepack that imprisoned the whales. Snow drifts became the underside of ice shelves carved out by the water currents by means of slide projections. Przybylski's attention to choreography was perhaps the most striking in the underwater sequences in which the whales and seals (large soft sculpture puppets) swam through the blue pool.

Marcel Pursued by the Hounds by Michel Tremblay (Tarragon Theatre and Pleiades Theatre, 1998)

The space designed itself. From the dramatic requirements of the play it was very clear that I had to find a strong place where two people could tell their stories and a mythical environment for the observing chorus of women. Our starting image was a Greek amphitheatre. It evolved into the sloping hills with lines and texture created by a maze of ropes, with the circle of a very small stage at the bottom. The chorus of women was physically isolated on the slopes, but with a perfect view into the world of Marcel and Thérèse below. The small size of Thérèse's room/circular platform helped to support an emotional bond between two main characters. The image of the hills and a small stage made the Tarragon stage spacious and claustrophobic at the same time. (TERESA PRZYBYLSKI)

The scenography for *Marcel Pursued by the Hounds* shows how Przybylski is prepared to create a fresh architectonics in a theatre. She imparted a monumentality to the post-industrial interior of the Mainspace at the Tarragon[8] by adapting her scenography from the concept of an amphitheatre. But instead of seating, this amphitheatre became a feature of the landscape that separated the two groups of characters. It appeared as the sand-coloured, bleached, and parched-earth embankment from an excavation that exposed an ancient and extensive root network. Visually this embankment filled the gap between the women on the upper level and the brother and sister on the lower level, but it also separated these characters conceptually in time and place. Przybylski transformed Tremblay's mise en scène of the three women seen knitting at the opening of the play into a hillside where tangled wool/rope became the elaborate root network holding the escarpment together. The three women on the upper level in their pale-coloured robes, with their connotations of costumes from ancient Greece, differed substantially in appearance from the two characters in contemporary dress on the lower level. Przybylski's scenography juxtaposed classical architecture to frame the action but realistic furnishings at its base: while the amphitheatre expressed the passage of time in centuries, the bed connoted time in decades. The set embodied the conceptual structure of Tremblay's play rather than physical details.

On the lower level, the bed disrupted the circularity of the amphitheatre. This bed became the abyss around which the characters moved, and in the spatial organization it eliminated the possibility of focussing the action in this central area. The total effect of the scenography was effectively disorienting, because in Tremblay's mise en scène both groups of characters reside in the Plateau, but in the spatial discontinuity of Przybylski's set these figures existed in different orders. This spatialization of tragic relationships through vertical juxtaposition of spaces opened new perspectives both on the play and in the Tarragon Theatre itself.

A Midsummer Night's Dream by William Shakespeare (Young People's Theatre, 1993)

> In the first stage of designing I let my right and left brain go loose. I let my hand draw what was hidden in my brain to evoke the dreaming, engage the unconscious and to make it into a visual image. This process was to make the mind fly freely, and to have the documents of that freedom. The original drawings evolved into new ideas, and in the end most of the images I discovered at the beginning were incorporated into one set. The costume design process was different. I knew that I would like to contrast the sharp white architectural shape of the court costumes with the soft black of the fairies. So the design process was to find the right shape in language that was concrete and architectural.
> (TERESA PRZYBYLSKI)

Przybylski removes the rational filters from a flow of images as she explores colours, textures, and shapes to develop a vocabulary for the production. Her focus is on the complex visual relationships between the density of the plastic elements and the movement of the performers. The preliminary sketches for *A Midsummer Night's Dream* are filled with expressions of physical energy within potential spaces for performance. In the watercolour sketches the distribution of colours and the abstraction of space tend to a fusion of background and foreground. In these sketches, images of phenomena that float in the air, shapes that emerge out of the darkness, define the sense of space and place. They stretch across the width of the stage or rise from the formlessness of an undefined floor. In an early design, lights and bubbles and eventually tiny faces hover over the intense magenta-coloured light on the floor, which illuminates them from below.

The overall effect of the costumes is developed by taking a Renaissance silhouette and reworking the relationships between the body and the materials. Strong angular features abstract the body of the actor and in each costume Przybylski emphasizes the upper body, with geometrically shaped hats and other headgear used to give special definition to the face. For the shoulders she develops a rigid structure that often leaves the arms free under it, and for some of the male figures she sketches elaborate overcoats. The costume sketches are done in pencil, and present a clear contrast in shapes on stage. Once Przybylski has established the shape for the costumes, she tries out colour combinations until she reaches the desired effect.

The Comedy of Errors by William Shakespeare (Tom Patterson Theatre, Stratford Festival, 1994, 1995)

Richard Rose who directed the *Comedy of Errors* wanted to work with an image of a modern society and to stress the timeless issues of the play. The most important part of the set was a series of freestanding light frames. Richard used the frames to create surprising illusions of walls and spaces. Movements of the frames were choreographed and became an important part of the action on stage. I was trying to avoid any direct references to any period in my costume designs. In my research I studied the paintings of Otto Dix and George Grosz, painters with an unusual and critical look at their contemporaries. In the final costume design I incorporated a lot of images from Dix's painting. (TERESA PRZYBYLSKI)

For this production in the Tom Patterson Theatre, the scenography had to incorporate the 40-foot thrust stage. Masking the dark wood of the upstage wall, Przybylski devised an imposing proscenium arch, the uprights of which were almost 2.5 feet wide and coloured a vivid blue. Instead of a proscenium curtain she suspended an 8-foot-wide plexiglass band that tapered to about 6 feet at the stage left edge. This trompe l'oeil solid structure substituted handily for a proscenium curtain, and drew attention to itself as if it were a fabric curtain left at a rakish angle by a failure of the curtain-raising machinery. Emphasizing its 'arrested' state, and to define its skewed angle, shading indicated a 'discrepancy' between various hems. The concept of the proscenium as a frame for the performance was repeated in three additional silverish-blue mobile frames, which diminished in size as they reached the outer edge of the thrust. These frames could be arranged on the stage to suggest rooms, corridors, and doorways. Przybylski's design exploited the thrust stage, encouraging the spectators to engage imaginatively in the production and conceive of the architectural planes of walls at the same time as these were absolutely transparent. This scenography maintained a focus on the stage at the height of the actors, while simultaneously invoking the narrative insistence on architecture. The frames could also be arranged so that, seen from a vantage point directly opposite the upstage wall, they fitted one inside another and reconfigured the thrust into a 'proscenium' theatre with a depth of 40 feet, the 'wings' of which were fully open to the view.[9]

Taking advantage of the proximity of the spectators, Przybylski enriched the costumes with details. Her sketches show each figure being incisively warped towards styles of social commentary evoking Otto Dix and George Grosz.[10] Satirical distortions achieved with padding, prosthetic devices, colour of fabric, and other elements are meant to fictionalize the performer's body: Doctor Pinch, painted in shades of green with accents of purple and yellow, is hunched around his belly, while his arms and legs are near skeletal; the sketches for the Gaoler and Officer are paired on a page to make a fine image of law enforcers – the Officer, with his barrel stomach contained by his jacket, has only a right hand, from which he dangles a pair of handcuffs, and the Gaoler in his zippered tunic holds his hands behind his back and balances on his left leg, the right one amputated at the knee and replaced by a crude wooden prosthesis. Przybylski also rhymes on the appearance of figures such as Luce and the Courtesan, inspired by Grosz's portraits of 'society.' The Courtesan is outfitted in a bright red, skintight, shiny vinyl dress, and Luce becomes the Dada-esque Tattooed Lady[11] whose corporeal bulk is expressed not in rolls of flesh but as three small drawers on the front of her dress. Przybylski's scenography effectively breaks with habitual social decorum on the stage, propelling the production into the darker regions of Shakespeare's *comédie humaine*.

The Emperor of Atlantis libretto by Petr Kien, composed by Viktor Ullman (Canadian Opera Company, Imperial Oil Theatre, Joey and Toby Tanenbaum Centre, 1998)

This opera evokes images of tragedy that is marginalized and forced. The venue for this production was a non-traditional theatre space with turn of the century strong industrial architecture. Even if there was no set, the production would be appropriate in that location. There were two issues that dominated the production: the story of the emperor of the mythical Atlantis and the real tragedy behind the original production that took place in the concentration camp in Theresienstadt. An island and a simple platform/stage, an old curtain, images of abandoned clothing and personal things conveyed the most important message of the opera: the tragedy of the Holocaust. (TERESA PRZYBYLSKI)

Przybylski's designs for *The Emperor of Atlantis* demonstrate her acute consciousness of the interaction between the venue and the particular work in her scenography.[12] The theatre space served as a metaphorical shell for a performance in which the stage was characterized as a makeshift platform. The spectators were made aware that Viktor Ullman had composed this opera in a concentration camp – in Terezin[13] – and she did not shy away from including allusions to the Holocaust; rather, she invited the spectators to speculate upon the circumstances under which opera, cabarets, and concerts might have taken place. Przybylski used the metaphor of an island, by choosing to make the spectator increasingly aware of the size of theatre.[14] In the vastness of the room she isolated the small playing space, and made this platform seem even more anomalous by surrounding it with the piles of discarded clothes. This eerily striking image was never referred to directly in the production and, along with the Machine for Death (one of the very few furnishings specified by the libretto), left the stage to the performers. The ramps for this stage platform expanded the playing space by making the singers visible as they approached. The provisional nature of the stage was continued in the upstage crossover, which looked like a hoarding fashioned out of bits of lumber and wall partitions commandeered for the event, and the back wall, which was partially masked by red fabric. The lighting of the production included footlights, which cast large shadows on the back wall of the 'Machine' mechanism and of the actors.

It was not until the closing moments of the opera that the theatre itself stood most fully revealed. One of the aspects of the room that Przybylski effectively integrated into the scenography was the ladder two-thirds of the way up the 37-foot-high wall. From this location a lone spectator – a guard – watched the performance. At the close of the performance he switched on a powerful searchlight to focus on the stage as the performers took their curtain call and were led off. At that moment a barbed wire curtain clanged down from the flies, incontrovertibly blocking any access to the stage from the auditorium; in the absence of actors, it transformed what had been a stage into a landscape of the concentration camp. A train whistle was heard, confirming for the spectators what they had suspected. Only seconds before, the footlights had been a source of illumination. Now, another penetrating beam was aimed directly out into the audience, well over the height of the stage. Across the empty stage the spectators faced the brick wall from which the red curtain had just been torn down, and on which the shadows of the performers had been cast.

Przybylski's watercolour sketches show how her strong scenographic concept began by establishing the idea of a makeshift theatre and proceeded to reveal the confines of the unadorned building. Her palette for the production contrasted the grey of the costumes and the stage with the pathetic attempt at theatrical opulence signified by the red cloth on the back wall. The costumes for this production were particularly remarkable for the way in which Przybylski investigated a monochromatic palette. The coats for the male figures, for example, although they were oversize and 'ill fitting,' served to emphasize the vitality of the singers. To move in these coats the singers had to exert a lot of energy and the effect was not only on the movement, but made a metaphoric link to the overall design in a prescient manner. If the characters discarded the coats, the figures on stage would not be easily differentiated and their garments would ironically contribute to the piles of clothes surrounding the stage. Przybylski brought together emblematic and functional props on the stage: a scythe for Death, and the faded traces of multi-coloured triangles sewn onto Harlequin's coat. These figures contrasted starkly with the hyper-realistic image of the soldier in his dehumanizing gas mask and military paraphernalia. The deeply considered simplicity of the scenography contemplated the expressions and meaning of a creativity unquenched by the Holocaust.

2nd Nature by Deanne Taylor (Hummer Sisters, Theatre Centre, 1990)

> This production offered a tremendous challenge. It was very complex. The small stage of the Theatre Centre had to accommodate projections and videos, support the story with several levels metaphorically and specifically and at the same time to be functional and safe for the actors. Deanne Taylor was very involved in the whole process of the design. We decided to use an ellipse as a configuration for the set because this shape offers a friendly perspective and the lines that can be drawn out of the ellipsoid shape contributed to organization of the space. Costumes for all the characters who impersonated parts of the human body and its functions were really fun to design. They had to be very clear to support the abstract concept of the play. (TERESA PRZYBYLSKI)

This scenography was part of a new initiative by the Hummer Sisters to take up performance in a theatre rather than a gallery or bar.[15] While the Hummer Sisters continued to use live and recorded video as they had been for over a decade,[16] Deanne Taylor also wanted to moderate the overwhelming presence of its mechanics in order to focus on the stage itself. Taylor also sought to bring indoors the narrative capacity of the visually dynamic costumes created by Trinidad artists for the Carnival.[17]

Teresa Przybylski's scenography met these challenges with its strong and dynamic visual rhythms. The set created an illusion of expansive breadth and height, its central ellipse inclined towards the spectators and rising to meet the line of the horizon. In the structure supporting the main ovoid ramp Przybylski embedded nineteen video monitors on two levels, each masked by a cardboard arch disguising the squareness of the monitor. Her sketch shows how the discrete shapes were designed to merge into each other in the perception of the spectator: the downstage edge of the ramp was an apparent continuation of the rounded shape of the cyclorama, and the openings for the monitors were echoed, although on a different scale and at a perpendicular angle, by the exit under the stage left ramp. An ink sketch precisely indicates how the well-defined edges of the all-black set were to be balanced by the flat expanses of the ramps and platforms.

The vivid colours of the costumes were even more vivid against the blackness of the set. While the main character was dressed in a simple silvery white costume,[18] the four 'organ sisters' were contemporary equivalents of the humours of the Renaissance stage, with identifying details integrated into the costume. Doc and Gusta both wore oversize necklaces: Doc's, indicating the immune system, was strung with medical paraphernalia; Gusta, representing appetite and the digestive system, wore garlands of large plastic fruit and vegetables. Cardia, representing the cardiovascular system, sported a large red majestic headdress, and Auto, 'the keeper of the glands, immune system and hormones,' wore a headdress and armbands that incorporated the colours of the other figures. These distinct costumes were highly articulate elements of the visual presentation.

Pinocchio by Maristella Roca (Young People's Theatre, 1993)

On this project I collaborated with Glen Davidson who designed the set. The images that Maristella [Roca] created in her play were extremely exciting and vivid, the stage directions were graphic and all we had to do was to accommodate them. It was very empowering from the first reading. For me the biggest practical challenge was the number of costume changes. With only 10 actors playing 40 characters, there was no time for elaborate changes. Together with the director Richard Greenblatt, we decided to assign one colour to each actor. Everyone received a specific colour costume base to which design pieces were added. In the final image the rainbow of complimentary colours seemed to enlarge the cast. I was very inspired by the play and enjoyed working on the practical solutions which resulted in a harmony of all aspects of the production. (TERESA PRZYBYLSKI)

Maristella Roca's adaptation[19] of Carlo Collodi's much-adapted novel brought the social criticism of the original onto the stage. In brief scenes, Roca seized on the novel's anti-authoritarian tone and working-class ethos. Przybylski's costumes matched the dramaturgy to various styles found in popular film and culture.

The colour scheme devised by Przybylski laid a foundation for the structure of the production. Her use of deep blue, orange, yellow, purple, and black ensured a lively mix of colours in all the scenes and demonstrated how she brings colour together with genre. As a highly menacing figure, the Cat, for instance, exhibited stark contrasts of streetwise glamour in black and white, right down to the high-top running shoes. More benign figures such as the water maidens in their different blue guises (Blue Girl I and II, the Blue Ass, Blue Dancer, Blue Water) were conceived according to shape rather than coded dress. With yet other characters, such as the Tunny, the Talking Ass, and Cricket group, Przybylski focussed on a bodily flexibility appropriate for dancer figures. Przybylski's costumes thus encouraged the young audiences to pay attention to various kinds of details – colour, props, and choreography – in reading the characters. Responding to the critical qualities of Roca's text, she distanced the production's visual presentation from storybook illustration.

Costume and set sketches by Teresa Przybylski confirm an imagination that works in three dimensions and a scenography that remains unfinished until the actors arrive. Her figures in the sketches express a dynamic energy. Pencil drawings such as 'Morgone' for *The Serpent Woman* (1991)[20] or 'Christobel Crum' for *1492* (1992)[21] demonstrate Przybylski's interest in experimenting with shape and space, whether it is on the page or on the stage. These large format drawings show not only how the details might be distributed in the costume, but the designer's imaginative engagement with the figures. Morgone's makeshift armour is created out of LP's wired together and the helmet fashioned out of borrowed materials (for the production this design was modified). The figure appears to have been squeezed into the confines of the sheet of paper. By contrast, Christopher Crum, as he sits off to one side of the page, gives the impression that he is emerging out of the page. Przybylski emphasizes Crum's concentration on the telescope and by his preoccupation gives the spectator license to peruse his image and see the how his clothes are holding the flesh from popping out. Her drawing picks up the subversive nature of mime, transgressing the rules of *politesse*. Przybylski's sketches contemplate the figure taking up space choreographically and gesturally. These two examples offer a good illustration of what Przybylski means when she says that her scenography seeks to 'find a space for things in production.'

NOTES

Introduction

1 The term and its connotations hark back to Vitruvius (Marcus Vitruvius Pollio) and his treatise *De Architectura* (written after 27 B.C.) in which scenography is one of three ways of representing a building in an architectural drawing, along with ichnography (the groundplan), and orthography (the front elevation). Scenography in Vitruvius is a representation of the front of a building with the sides withdrawing into the background and in which all the lines meet in the centre of a circle. He did not apply the term to the theatre directly but employed this principle of perspective when he discussed the proportions of the *scaena* relative to the spectators and how to make theatre architecture sufficiently imposing as a civic building.

   When Sebastiano Serlio translated Vitruvius in the sixteenth century, his use for 'scenography' was related to perspectival paintings of buildings used as two-dimensional backdrops on the stage. As Christopher S. Wood points out, 'scenography' at this time had 'a broader sense, for it can denote quite generally the application of optical laws to the visual art and architecture in their entirety: that is not only the rules for making flat pictures on flat surfaces, but also the rules of architectonic and plastic construction, insofar as the latter are interested in countering the distortions entailed in the process of seeing' (see Panofsky, *Perspective as Symbolic Form*, 97).

2 Svoboda, *The Secret of Theatrical Space*, 14.

3 The initials of the name in French serve as the name of the organization in English.

4 At the Stratford Festival Tanya Moiseiwitsch, Desmond Heeley, Brian Jackson, and Leslie Hurry dominated the design for productions of Shakespeare until the early 1970s. Kay Ambrose, who came to Canada with Celia Franca to found the National Ballet, was the resident designer for the first decade. Similarly the Canadian Opera Company was largely under the artistic control of Herman Geiger-Torel for its first eight years, who with his experience of opera in Europe and the United States contracted designers with experience elsewhere, and the Royal Winnipeg Ballet also initially relied on designers from abroad.

5 Mark Negin started the design department at the National Theatre School with Robert Prévost in 1961.

6 See Patricia Adams's invaluable mimeographed compilation *Stage Designers of Canada*. In her introduction Adams points out that a full record of the designers' work was impossible since neither the theatres nor the designers themselves had systematic records.

7 *Report: Royal Commission on National Development in the Arts, Letters and Sciences 1949–1951*. The introduction by S. Marchbanks (aka Robertson Davies) characterized the inadequacy of the typical Canadian 'theatre': 'Nine times out of ten, Fishorn, it is a school hall, smelling of chalk and kids, and decorated in Early Concrete style. The stage is a small, raised room at one end. And I mean room. If you step into the wings suddenly you will fracture your nose against the wall. There is no place for storing scenery, no place for the actors to dress, and the light is designed to warm the stage but not to illuminate it' (192).

8 'A few Canadian universities have full-time departments of drama, and in such summer schools as the Banff

School of Fine Arts much excellent work is being done. But nowhere in Canada does there exist advanced training for the playwright, the producer, the technician or the actor; nor does it seem rational to advocate the creation of suitable schools of dramatic art in Canada when present prospects for the employment in Canada of the graduates seem so unfavourable' (Recommendation 10, *Report*, 196).

9 'We have been repeatedly informed that the theatre could be revived if only federal subsidies could be secured for the erection of suitable playhouses throughout Canada and for part of the travelling expenses of Canadian professional companies. We have also been told that a chain of legitimate theatres throughout Canada would make possible tours of competent professional companies from abroad, thus providing a stimulus to Canadian actors and playwrights and a useful example of the wide gulf separating the interested amateur from the competent professional who has been thoroughly trained and apprenticed, learning his craft under the goad of sternly skilful direction and of ruthless competition ... *Les Compagnons de St-Laurent* agreed with the Western Stage Society that the construction of theatres and halls on a grand scale is not necessary or advisable but that much could be done to make existing accommodation more suitable for theatrical performances if competent advice on the matter were available from a central agency' (Recommendation 11, *Report*, 197).

10 For an account of the personal excitement engendered by the founding of the theatre see Ferry, 'Experience of a Pioneer in Canadian Experimental Theatre,' 59–67.

11 Workshop Productions set out to give actor training in a more physical style of theatre based in the work of Rudolf Laban. See Carson, *Harlequin in Hogtown*, 24–7.

12 Ibid., 31–2.

13 Tyrone Guthrie was very specific about the way the architectural stage designed by Tanya Moiseiwitsch was employed during the first season: 'The designer's aim was to offer the facilities of an Elizabethan stage, but not to attempt an Elizabethan pseudo-style. The floor was of oak, polished – about as shiny as a dance floor; the pillars, balcony and partition wall were stained a rather darker colour, appreciably darker than the actors' faces. The general visual effect we aimed at was to be strictly "functional"; neither aggressively modern nor antique; a structure that unobtrusively offered to the actors standing-places, seats, and things to lean against, when they needed them; a platform that offered neither too much space nor too little, and which was so placed as to be the focal point of the nearly circular auditorium.

'There was no curtained alcove under the balcony, partly because I did not think which of these two plays required its use (and I am not convinced that this practicality is, in fact, a necessity), partly because we did not like the look of drapery in this position.

'Because we played at night, artificial light was a necessity. But there were no illusionary "effects" of light. We permitted ourselves an unobtrusive "dim" at what seemed appropriate times, not without feeling that this was a weak concession to current theatrical convention and a departure from a method and style we had adopted.

'Scenic austerity was offset by extremely rich and handsome clothes.' Guthrie, 'Shakespeare at Stratford, Ontario,' 128.

14 The Garrick, dating from 1915. For the excitement of creating the Neptune Theatre see Bruce, *Happy Birthday, Dear Neptune*.

15 The 2,326-seat Opera, the 969-seat Theatre, the 350-seat Studio, and the 150-seat Salon.

16 The Avon Theatre was initially used for musical theatre and opera designed mainly by the designers who worked on the Festival stage.

17 Quoted in Perkyns, *The Neptune Story*, 14, 16.

18 Neil Carson describes Luscombe's search for an appropriate space that would take into account the surrounding community. See Carson, *Harlequin*, 75–7. TWP ceased operation in 1992 and the space was taken over by Buddies in Bad Times Theatre.

19 There were two theatres: the upstairs space had a stage 29 feet × 20 feet with seating for about 180, and the downstairs space stage was 50 feet × 21 feet with seating for 280. See Johnston, *Up the Mainstream*, 180.

20 In 1991 this third stage, now a permanent resource of the Festival, was named the Tom Patterson Theatre.

21 When they re-opened in 1983 the larger theatre was renamed the Bluma Appel Theatre and in 1985 the Town

Hall, the smaller of the two, was renamed Jane Mallett Theatre. The capacity of the Bluma Appel was increased from 830 to 890 seats. Theatre boxes were introduced and the rake in the auditorium was greatly decreased. The original stage, which could be configured as a proscenium, thrust, or triptych surrounding the audience, was replaced by a retractable proscenium arch with a forestage that could be lowered to accommodate an orchestra pit.

22 Five years later, this small space was enlarged to seat 140 and hold the company's office.

23 Nineteen countries sent delegations in that inaugural year.

24 Robert Prévost was the most experienced of the designers, since he had been working as a designer since 1949. Among his credits were designs for Les Compagnons de St Laurent, Le Rideau vert, Le Théâtre du Nouveau Monde, the Canadian Opera Company, the National Ballet of Canada, the Royal Winnipeg Ballet, and also for television series on Radio Canada (this television division was the forerunner of the Canadian Broadcasting Corporation in Quebec). With Mark Negin he started the design program at the National Theatre School.

25 Michael Eagan graduated from the National Theatre School in 1967 and had been designing in the English- and French-language theatres in the Montreal area, the Centaur, Festival Lennoxville, the Saidye Bronfman Centre, La Compagnie Jean Duceppe, as well as the National Arts Centre in Ottawa, Theatre Plus in Toronto, and Theatre New Brunswick in Fredericton. He had also worked in film and television. He would later become the head of the design program of the National Theatre School.

26 Susan Benson's work is the focus of chapter 2, below.

27 Cameron Porteous had extensive experience in television and film. He was the head of design at the Vancouver Playhouse and had been appointed associate director of the theatre. He had also taught design at the Banff School of Fine Arts. He would later become head of design at the Shaw Festival.

28 Astrid Janson's designs are the focus of chapter 1, below.

29 Beaupré, ed., *Theatre Design Explorations/ Scénographie au Canada*, [2].

30 'Astrid Janson' in ibid., [7].

31 'Susan Benson' in ibid., [5].

32 The designers were Susan Benson, Raymond-Marius Boucher, Sean Breaugh, Mérédith Caron, Charlotte Dean, Lance Dutrizac, Julie Fox, Robert Gardiner, Kathleen Irwin, John Jenkins, Shawn Kerwin, Michael Levine, Ken MacDonald, Brian Perchaluk, Peter Perina, Christina Poddubiuk, Cameron Porteous, Teresa Przybylski, Robert Shannon, Ed Sharp, Phillip Silver, Carolyn M. Smith, Allan Stichbury, and Ange Zhang.
   Cameron Porteous was the curator of this exhibit as well as the one of the previous delegation in 1994. The exhibit was featured as part of the du Maurier World Stage Theatre Festival at Harbourfront in Toronto in 1998, and transferred to during the Rothmans Gallery, Stratford, under the title 'Stage Design in Canada: 1994–1998.'

33 Quoted from the one-page brochure produced by the ADC addressing the larger exhibit and the delegation to Prague.

34 The Dora Mavor Moore Awards were established in Toronto in 1981; the Jessie Richardson Theatre Awards were established in Vancouver in 1983; and the Sterling Awards, in honour of Elizabeth Sterling Haynes, were established in Edmonton in 1987.

35 No. 70 (1992) focussed on scenography and 91 (1997) took up designer training in Canada.

36 See Gallery/Stratford, *Made Glorious: Twenty-Five Years of Design*; Gallery/Stratford, *From Sketch to Stage*; *Designs for Theatre: Stratford Festival, 1954–1990*; *A 10th Season Souvenir Collection of Costume Designs from the Stratford Festival*; *Souvenir Costume Designs from the Stratford Festival*.

37 See Shaw Festival, *The Pictorial Stage: Twenty Five Years of Vision and Design at the Shaw Festival*, published to accompany an exhibition at the Niagara Historical Society Museum, Niagara-on-the-Lake, 11 June to 28 September 1986. Holmes, *Celebrating! Twenty-Five Years at the Shaw Festival*.

38 Dafoe, *Dancing through Time*.

39 Mercedes Palomino, Guilermo de Andrea, and Serge Turgeon, *Le Théâtre du Rideau Vert: 50 ans à célébrer le théâtre, 1949–1999*.

40 Patricia Belzil and Solange Lévesque, *L'Album du Théâtre du Nouveau Monde*.

41 Bouchard, *L'art de la scène: passé-présent: scénographie québécoise, 1940–1990*, the first of these volumes, is a photographic record made up of archival photos. The second volume, *L'Espace théâtral: portrait de la création scénographique 1991–1994*, is a catalogue from an exhibit of more recent work. It features pictures of maquettes or drawings alongside production photos to bring into the discussion the process of scenographic design. This exhibit followed on a critical engagement with scenographic design in the early 1990s.

42 Jean-François Chassay et al., *L'Album du Théâtre Ubu: Mises en scène de Denis Marleau, 1982–1994*.

43 *La scénographie au Québec*, special issue of *L'Annuaire théâtral* 11 (1992) and *Enquête sur la scénographie québecoise* and *'Scénographie' and 'Scénographie'-suite*, special issues of *Les Cahiers de théâtre jeu*, 10 (1979) and 62 (1992).

1 Astrid Janson

1 She designed costumes for *Baroque Suite* by David Earle (1972), *Lacemakers* by Barry Smith (1972), *Boat, River, Moon* by David Earle (1972), *Three Sided Room* by Peter Randazzo (1972), *The Last Act* by Peter Randazzo (1972), *Los Sencillos* by Patricia Beatty (1972), *Figure in the Pit* by Peter Randazzo (1973), *Ray Charles Suite* by David Earle (1973), *Atlantis* by David Earle (1973), *Harold Morgan's Delicate Balance* by Patricia Beatty (1973), *A Walk in Time* by Peter Randazzo (1973), *A Flight of Spiral Stairs* by Peter Randazzo (1973), and *Babar* by Donald Hines (when the show was planned for the St Lawrence Centre, 1973).

2 Janson designed fifteen productions for TWP between 1974 and 1982. Among them was *Ten Lost Years* by Barry Broadfoot, adapted by Jack Winter and Cedric Smith (1974), a show that TWP toured extensively in Canada (as late as 1981) and to Europe (1976).

3 During this very dynamic and busy period of her career her two children were born.

4 Among her designs for the CBC were the premiere season of *King of Kensington*, episodes of *Home Fires* and *The Tommy Hunter Show*, and several programs in the Super Special Series, which featured Canadian performers such as figure skater Toller Cranston and singer Anne Murray. She also designed several adaptations of plays.

5 For the Shaw Festival, Janson designed the costumes for Shaw's *Captain Brassbound's Conversion* (Festival Theatre, 1979), the set and costumes for Chekhov's *The Cherry Orchard* (Festival Theatre, 1980) and Shaw's *Candida* (Court House Theatre, 1983).

6 For the Stratford Festival, Janson designed the costumes for Gilbert and Sullivan's *HMS Pinafore* (Avon Theatre, 1981).

7 In the Tom Patterson Theatre she has designed Eugene O'Neill's *Long Day's Journey into Night* (1994, 1995), Timothy Findley's *Stillborn Lover* (1995) and Tennessee Williams's *Sweet Bird of Youth* (1996). She has also designed Shakespeare's *Othello* for the Festival Theatre (1987) and costumes for Arthur Miller's *Death of a Salesman* in the Avon Theatre (1998).

8 Eugene O'Neill's *A Moon for the Misbegotten* at the Tarragon Theatre (1985) and *The Grace of Mary Traverse* by Timberlake Wertenbaker at the Toronto Free Theatre (1987). In the latter design the stylized period costumes incorporated animal figures as metaphorical equivalents to character. There are no extant sketches or pictures from this production.

9 Janson designed the set for Edward Albee's *Three Tall Women* in 1996.

10 An association of professional actors in Toronto, Theatre Compact presented two seasons, renting space at Toronto Workshop Productions and the Bathurst Street Theatre. Janson designed Hugh Leonard's *Da* (1976), Nicolas Erdman's *The Suicide* (1976), and Strindberg's *Easter* (1977).

11 Global Village operated a theatre in a warehouse on St Nicholas Street from 1969 to 1975. Janson designed costumes for two of their productions, Robert Swerdlow's *Glorification* (1973) and Malcolm Mills and Elizabeth Swerdlow's *Hey Justine* (1974).

12 Frank Wedekind's *Lulu* (1977), Ibsen's *The Master Builder* (1983), Michel Tremblay's *Albertine in Five Times* (1985, and tour in 1986), Eugene O'Neill's *A Moon for the Misbegotten* (1985), and John Murrell's *October* (1988).

13 Mordecai Richler's *Jacob Two-Two and the Hooded Fang* (1984, 1985, 1987) and *Jacob Two-Two and the Dinosaur* (1989, and remounted at the Citadel Theatre in Edmonton, 1989).

14 James Kudelka's *Playhouse* (1980), *Musings* (1991), and *Vittoria Pas de deux* (1993); *Portrait of Love and Death* by Vincente Nebrada (1982).

15 Costumes for *Firebird Suite* by Vincente Nebrada (1982). Her designs for this production were particularly notable, since they were a hybrid between costuming and puppet creation. She provided the illusion of many more figures on stage than just the twenty dancers by adding heads, as gigantic gloves, to increase the number of creatures on stage to thirty-four.

16 René Aloma's *A Little Something to Ease the Pain* (1980).

17 *Cabaret*, music by John Kander and lyrics by Fred Ebb (1983). Janson's design sketches for this production resembled the drawings of Georg Grosz. See Special Collections, Toronto Reference Library.

18 *Incognito* by Robert Desrosiers for the Winter Olympics in Calgary (1988).

19 *Charming and Rose* by Kelly Jo Burke (Theatre Centre, 1993), *Harlem Duet* by Djanet Sears (Downstairs Theatre at Berkeley Street, 1997).

20 Costumes for *Tory, Tory, Tory* (1983), *The Great Debate* (1993), *Vox Pop* (1993), *Canada or Can't* (1998), and *The History of the Village of the Small Huts* (1992 to 1997).

21 Anton Dvořák's *Rusalka* (1988).

22 Rossini's *The Barber of Seville* (1992).

23 By Kelly Jo Burke (Nightwood Theatre, Theatre Centre, 1993).

24 By Stephen Sondheim (Canadian Stage, Bluma Appel Theatre, St Lawrence Centre, 1997).

25 By Henrik Ibsen (Tarragon Theatre, 1983).

26 The original set was destroyed by fire in the theatre on the night of 4 November 1974. The production opened several weeks later on 31 December in the Alexander Street theatre.

27 Carson, *Harlequin in Hogtown*, 136.

28 Janson has used this technique several times: 'In *Esmeralda, and the Hunchback of Notre Dame* by Andrew Piotrowski and George Luscombe (1978) there were over a hundred puppets, and they functioned as a physical presence of the crowd witnessing the humiliation of the Hunchback and also as a symbolic presentation of characters. Different construction techniques were used: the police were straw people, the lepers were part dummy worn by the actors, and the Bishop was on stilts. In *Cabaret* by Joe Masteroff (Centre Stage, 1983) puppets were danced with, and they made the Kit Kat Klub look crowded, and they were able to heighten the caricature of the characters who were there. I used them to go the next step with extreme caricature, by their position, their attitude, or by actions – that human actors could only suggest – they became more extreme than the human actors and could even be treated in a violent way – thrown across the floor without endangering the actors. As well as helping to establish class and the symbolism of character, these figures allow strong non-representational theatre out of time' (Astrid Janson).

29 The weekly radio and television broadcasts of the hockey games by the Canadian Broadcasting Corporation.

30 *The Great War* (1992), *The Life and Times of Mackenzie King* (1993), and *World War II* (1994), all by Michael Hollingsworth.

31 *The Cold War* (1995), *Trudeau and the FLQ* (1996), and *Trudeau and the PQ* (1997), all by Michael Hollingsworth.

32 Jim Plaxton designed the black box. See discussion in chapter 4 below.

33 Productions such as *The Great Debate*, *Canada or Can't* (1995), or *VideoCabaret News* (1998), or other cabarets brought live video with recorded footage from television together with live performance. The actors in these productions took the roles of reporters and studio anchors.

34 *The Cherry Orchard*, Costume bible, Shaw Festival Archives.

35 For O'Neill's *Long Day's Journey into Night* in this theatre (1994, 1995), Janson used this upstage area to include the stairs to the second floor so that Mary Tyrone's retreat could be made emphatic. Mary's presence, even when not on stage, was presented to the audience by a soundscape of footsteps. A ceiling cloth produced a hyper-real atmosphere of a fog permeating the house. She balanced these areas of the stage by making the wicker furniture a 'dust' colour to be absorbed by the atmosphere in the house.

2 Susan Benson

1 The Krannert Center was built on the Urbana-Champaign campus in 1969. It comprises the Tyron Festival

Theatre (seating 979), the Colwell Playhouse (seating 674), and the black box studio (seating 200). The complex has extensive backstage and workshop space.

2 For the 1974 season Susan Benson designed *The Summoning of Everyman* by Anonymous and Menotti's opera *The Medium* for this theatre.

3 Costumes for Ibsen's *A Doll's House* (1996).

4 Benson designed costumes for *Steps* by Brian Macdonald, which the Royal Winnipeg Ballet premiered at Expo '86.

5 Costumes for *L'Île inconnue* by Constanin Patsalas (1983), set and costumes for John Cranko's *Taming of the Shrew* (1991) and Boston Ballet (1995), and *Romeo and Juliet* (1995) and the National Ballet of Helsinki (1996).

6 Mozart's *Marriage of Figaro* (1990) and *Cosi fan tutti* (1991).

7 Mozart's *La Finta Giardiniera* at the Guelph Spring Festival and at the St Louis Opera (1987).

8 Costumes for Verdi's *La Forza del Destino* (1987), Benjamin Britten's *Death in Venice* (1984) and in San Francisco (1997), set and costumes for Puccini's *Madama Butterfly* (1990, 1994, 1998), and *The Golden Ass* by Gary Kulesha and libretto by Robertson Davies (1999).

9 Costumes for Massenet's *Don Quichotte* (1986).

10 Mozart's *The Magic Flute*, a co-production with the Dallas Opera (1997).

11 Gilbert and Sullivan's *The Gondoliers* (1989).

12 *Design Made Glorious* was an exhibit to celebrate the Stratford Festival's twenty-fifth anniversary.

13 This was the second grant Benson had received from the Canada Council: in 1970 she was awarded an artist's grant.

14 Lacy Baldwin Smith, *The Horizon Book on the Elizabethan World* (New York: American Heritage, 1976) and Roy Strong, *The Elizabethan Image: Painting in England, 1540–1620*, Tate Gallery Exhibition Catalogue (London, 1969) were sources for the *mises en scène*. See Knowles, 'Robin Phillips' Strange and Wondrous Dream,' 38–58.

15 The staging of these well-known American musicals in the Festival Theatre was a bold move made by John Neville, the artistic director. The widespread interest in musicals in Toronto did not begin in earnest until 1990s, though there were some earlier productions, such as *Cabaret* by the Centre Stage Company at the St Lawrence Centre in 1983. In Toronto, *Cats* had played at the Elgin Theatre from 1981 to 1987; *Phantom of the Opera* opened at the Pantages Theatre in 1989; *Wizard of Oz* played at the Elgin in 1989.

16 Brian Macdonald, 'The Work of a Designer,' in *Susan Benson Artist/Designer* Exhibition Catalogue, [4].

17 Susan Benson's successful collaboration on *The Mikado* with Brian Macdonald as director led to their work together on subsequent productions of Gilbert and Sullivan, as well as to designs for *Madama Butterfly* for the Canadian Opera Company (1990), *Steps* at the Royal Winnipeg Ballet (1986), *Cabaret* at the Festival Theatre (1987) and *Guys and Dolls* at the Festival Theatre (1990).

18 At Stratford Susan Benson also designed *The Gondoliers* (1983/1984, 1995), *Iolanthe* (1984), *The Pirates of Penzance* (1994), and *H.M.S. Pinafore* (1988, 1992). She also designed *The Gondoliers* (1989) for the Australian Opera Company.

19 The Avon Theatre had been used for tours of companies performing Gilbert and Sullivan during the early sixties. When the Festival took over the Avon Theatre several productions were mounted by the Festival, but the theatre was used primarily for productions of opera.

20 The D'Oyly Carte's rights to Gilbert and Sullivan had run out in 1961, and revivals in London as well as on Broadway were looking for a fresh approach.

21 The fan was introduced at a late stage in the development of the design when Douglas A. McLean, Benson's co-designer of the set, brought the hand fan to her office and they set it into the maquette for the set.

22 *The Mikado* (1982), Susan Benson, Stage Designs, Special Collections, Toronto Reference Library.

23 These upstage tableaux conjured up the images of the *fêtes galantes* painted by Watteau in which being outdoors is celebrated by bringing nymphs, Venus, and cupids together with human figures. *The Venetian Festival* and *La Conversation* by Watteau are examples of the style.

24 Jürgen Rose was the designer for several ballets choreographed by John Cranko, including *Romeo and Juliet* when it was mounted by the Stuttgart Ballet in 1962, and when it went on tour to the Metropolitan Opera

House in New York in 1969. This production first came into the repertoire of the National Ballet of Canada in 1964. His costumes for the chorus, in particular, were made up of vivid reds, oranges, and olive greens with strong dark accents and outlines to emphasize the individual components of the costumes. He also used heavier fabric throughout his design for the chorus.

25 Benson's design for the Stratford *Taming of the Shrew* (1981) put Katherine in a costume that was demonstratively hand-painted and quilted to reinforce the floral pattern at the hem. It was almost a picture come to life. In performance, it contributed to the presentation of Katherine as a kind of Galatea to Petruchio's Pygmalion.

26 Reid Anderson, who had danced in the original production at the Stuttgart Ballet and directed this production, appreciated the aesthetic implications of Benson's refinement in the structure of the bridge and adjusted the choreography to exploit it.

27 *Romeo and Juliet* costume bible, Archives, National Ballet of Canada.

3 Mary Kerr

1 Rudakoff, 'Mary Kerr: In Conversation,' 5.

2 She graduated with a BFA (Honours) in 1966. Her thesis show was a series of large sculptures that celebrated the female body in wall sculpture, oversize marionettes, free-standing sculpture, and grafts onto a found object – a guitar.

3 The PLS was formed in 1965 in the Centre for Medieval Studies as a means to study medieval plays through performance.

4 Kerr designed Shaw's *The Admirable Bashville* in the Court Theatre at the Shaw Festival (1974); Voltaire's *Candide* in the Avon Theatre at the Stratford Festival (1978); *Desert Song* by Otto Harbach, Oscar Hammerstein, and Frank Mandel and Shaw's *The Music Cure* in the Royal George Theatre at the Shaw Festival (1982); Noel Coward's *Private Lives* in the Festival Theatre at the Shaw Festival (1983); and *Once in a Lifetime* by Moss Hart and George S. Kauffman in the Festival Theatre at the Shaw Festival (1988).

5 Mozart's *Fidelio* (1978).

6 Benjamin Britten's *The Turn of the Screw* (1988).

7 In New Zealand in 1986, on an Arts Grant B for Cultural Exchange from the Canada Council, she designed Stephen Sondheim's *Sweeney Todd* and Puccini's *Tosca*.

8 Two ballets with choreography by Jacques Lemay: *The Big Top: A Circus Ballet* (1986) and her own scenario and design for *Anne of Green Gables* (1989).

9 Jacques Lemay's *The Tin Soldier* (1989).

10 Her first design for a political cabaret was *Orang-Utan* in the tiny space of the Theatre in the Dell in 1974. She later undertook designs for Salome Bey's tour of *Indigo*; *Captivating Cole* at the Grand Theatre in London, Ontario, in 1984; and the costumes for the musical review at the Deerhurst Inn in 1990.

11 Exhibition notes for Exhibition by Associated Designers of Canada, 1979. Mary Kerr Collection, box 1, envelope 6, Special Collections, Toronto Reference Library. The curator of this exhibit at Hart House, University of Toronto, was Martha Mann. The work of sixteen designers from across Canada was featured.

12 Mary Kerr Collection, box 1, envelope 6, notes to *The Stag King*.

13 Natalia Goncharova designed costumes for Serge Diaghilev's Ballets Russes in Paris from 1914 to 1926.

14 Ivan Bilibin (1876–1942), illustrator of Russian folk tales. He was a designer for the 'Russian Opera Season' in Paris in 1927. His illustrations of Oriental and Russian folk tales and monumental moments in history are notable for the black outlines of individual details in a picture, the juxtaposition of blocks of colour that gives the impression of a two dimensionality, and the emphasis on terrain. Such is his emphasis on the Russian forests as the setting for the fairy tales that the trees are often drawn with the same detail and on the same scale as the human figures.

15 See Frank Lloyd Wright, 'An Architect Speaking for Culture' (1936), 'An Organic Architecture' (1939) and *An Autobiography* (1943). He rejected the purely functional geometry of 'post and beam' construction in favour of

integrating the structural aspects with the aesthetics of a building. He advocated merging the lines of walls, ceilings, and floors, so that they became 'not only party to each other but *part of each other*, reacting and within one another' (Frank Lloyd Wright, 'Organic Architecture' [1936] in *Frank Lloyd Wright on Architecture: Selected Writings*, edited by, Frederick Gutheim [New York: Universal Library, Grosset and Dunlap, 1941] 182). To achieve such an effect of continuity he advocated rethinking how materials were to be deployed and therefore needed to be *seen*, insisting that such organic plasticity in architecture emphasized the relationship between the plastic elements – wood (natural), metal, and synthetic materials such as concrete (Frank Lloyd Wright, *An Autobiography* [New York: Duell, Sloan, and Pearce, 1943], 147). The point of departure for his designs was the horizontal line, which he termed the line of repose, and from which all design could grow.

16 Rudakoff, 'Mary Kerr,' 5.

17 Erwin Piscator (1893–1966) and Max Reinhardt (1873–1943) were two *metteurs en scène* whose rejection of naturalism led to productions in which the presence of the performer was in a dynamic relationship with the aesthetic contexts.

18 Mary Kerr Collection, box 4, envelope 16.

19 Note to Ihor Sychylo at Banff Centre for the Arts, 17 October 1988, Mary Kerr Collection, box 4, envelope 12.

20 Constructivists such as Vladimir Tatlin, Alexandra Exter and El Lissitzky referred to the 'expressive life' of materials such as wood and metal as 'faktura' and used it to emphasize the way in which materials were being deployed to create geometric or abstract constructions.

21 Correspondence and production records, Mary Kerr Collection, box 4, envelopes 17–18.

22 The influence of such Constructivist designers as Vladimir Stenberg, Kazimir Malevich (and his suprematist experiments in colour and costumes), and Alexandra Exter is evident, but where the sketches by these designers abstract the bodies into purely geometric form, Kerr draws plausibly human figures.

Kerr had used the same colour scheme in the production of Bertolt Brecht's *Jungle of the Cities* at the Toronto Free Theatre (1983) but the effect was substantially different in this earlier production, since its asymmetrical costumes were designed to suggest animal equivalents for each character, and their geometry to interact with the angularity of the scaffolding.

23 Kerr used a typeface developed by Le Corbusier which he used in the stencil to title his drawings. Kerr found Charette retailed by Lettraset as an equivalent. Mary Kerr Collection, box 4, envelope 10.

24 Kerr's imagery was inspired by the final lines of one of Wordsworth's *Lucy* poems, 'A slumber did my spirit seal': 'Rolled round in earth's diurnal course, / With rocks and stones and trees.'

25 Exhibition Notes for Associated Designers of Canada 1979, Mary Kerr Collection, box 1, envelope 6.

26 Mary Kerr had collaborated closely with director Stephen Katz from the late 1960s to the mid-1980s, when he moved to the United States. Their work together included Carlo Gozzi's *The Stag King* (Tarragon, 1972), Machiavelli's *La Mandragola* (Vancouver Playhouse, 1974), and *The Desert Song*, book and lyrics by Otto Harbach, Oscar Hammerstein, and Frank Mandel, with music by Sigmund Romberg (Shaw Festival, 1983).

27 The design for these and other costumes presented an interesting interplay of colour and function that was highly reminiscent of the sports clothes designed by Russian Constructivist designers of the 1920s such as Varvara Stepanova.

28 Mary Kerr Collection, box 1, envelope 6.

29 Mary Kerr, personal correspondence.

30 Many of Kerr's designs can be seen in the photographs of Danny Grossman's company by Cylla von Tiedemann. See Cylla von Tiedemann, *The Dance Photography of Cylla von Tiedemann*.

31 Chagall had created various paintings of lovers: *Lovers in Blue* (1914), *Lovers with Flowers* (1927), *Lovers in Lilac* (1930), and *Bouquet with Flying Lovers* (1934–47).

32 In earlier works such as *Higher* (1977) Kerr used a ladder and a chair for the dancers to move on and through.

33 Notably in Shaw and Stratford shows of the 1970s.

34 Sonia Delaunay (1885–1979) had been creating *robes simultanées* in which colour and form work independently of the shape of the body. The costume displayed its own geometry of circles and squares in contrast to the potential choreography. The choice by Kerr of simultaneous costume for Tzara is apt, since Delaunay designed the costumes for Tzara's *Coeur à gaz* in 1923.

35 Jean Cocteau subtitled *Parade* to make explicit that the dance was 'not the result of an effort to achieve decorative effects, but of a desire to amplify the real, to introduce the detail of daily truths and rhythms into the vocabulary of dancing' (Jean Cocteau, '*Parade*: Ballet réaliste,' *Vanity Fair*, September 1917. Quoted in Frank W. Ries, *The Dance of Jean Cocteau* [Ann Arbor, MI: UMI, 1986], 188).

36 The term is taken from the work of Futurists Fortunato Depero (1892–1960), and Enrico Prampolini (1894–1960), who advocated costumes as scenery, and whose philosophy was clearly operative in this production.

37 Meyerhold's *The Death of Tarelkin* was designed by Varvara Stepanova in 1922. The production was famous for its references to the cabaret and vaudeville in the playing style and neutrality of costumes.

38 Kerr created the caribou figures by extending the arms of the costumes into hoofed feet, so that the manipulators walked on all fours.

4 Jim Plaxton

1 Alan Watts, 'Sculptured Spaces: Jim Plaxton in conversation with Alan Watts,' 54.

2 The Three Schools of Art was the amalgamation of the Artists' Workshop, the Hockley Valley Art School, and the New School of Art, which shared premises on Markham Street from 1966 until 1970, when they moved to the Poor Alex at 296 Brunswick Avenue. Run by John Simes, the Schools offered courses in visual and performing arts, crafts, and writing.

3 Watts, 'Sculpured Spaces,' 55.

4 Toronto Dance Theatre was formed in 1968. Initially Plaxton worked with Toronto Dance Theatre as a set and lighting designer; three years later, in 1971, he became the company's first official administrator and was instrumental in organizing its first tour to England in the spring of 1972. The film of *Encounter* is in the CBC Archives. In addition to *Encounter* Plaxton served as lighting designer and designed sets for several other works by Peter Randazzo: *Continuum* (1969), *I Had Two Sons* (1970), *Visions for a Theatre of the Mind* (1971), *Prospect Park* (1971), as well as *Portrait* (1970) and *The Silent Feast* (1971) by David Earle.

5 The play was adapted and directed by Ernest Schwartz, Studio Lab's artistic director. The production toured Ontario before settling into a five-week run at the Bathurst Street Theatre.

6 Le Corbusier in *Vers une Architecture* (1923) emphasized the house as part of the structure of society, so that buildings were not refuges, but ways of encountering the environment – 'machines for living in.' The International Style of architecture advocated by Le Corbusier and Walter Gropius of the Bauhaus School stressed the conception of a total visual environment which emphasized form following function, planes highlighted by lighting, and accentuated the use of materials and geometry in construction. See Hanno-Walter Kruft, *A History of Architectural Theory: From Vitruvius to the Present* (London: Zwemmer; New York: Princeton Architectural Press, 1994), 397–9.

7 Shaw's *Too True to be Good!* (1981). The designs for this production were part of the Canadian exhibit at the Prague Quadrennial in 1983.

8 Located in the basement of the Hart House on the campus of the University of Toronto, the theatre has a proscenium arch of 30 feet × 15 feet and a stage 22 feet deep. It was commissioned by the Massey Foundation in 1919. Plaxton was the resident lighting designer for three seasons from 1978 to 1982, during which time the theatre was an integral part of the Graduate Centre for the Study of Drama.

9 Clarke Rogers succeeded Paul Thompson as the new artistic director of Theatre Passe Muraille in 1982. The change in artistic direction also meant a shift in policy: during Paul Thompson's tenure the theatre emphasized collective creations; under Clarke Rogers the theatre began to produce more scripted plays.

10 Theatre Passe Muraille had moved into its permanent residence at 16 Ryerson Street in 1975 but four years later it had still received only enough funding to complete minimal renovations. The building housed three theatres: the Backspace was a pocket-size theatre of 704 square feet and steeply banked bleacher seating for 65; the second storey of the main section accommodated a performance space 56 feet × 70 feet seating 250; and on the ground floor, from which offices and washrooms were carved out, was a performance space smaller than the one above it.

11 The play was written by Clarke Rogers under the pseudonym Claude Roberts.

12 Rogers and Plaxton had originally conceived the destruction of the apartment as signalling the mental and moral deterioration of the characters. This concept was rejected after the first public performance, in which furniture disintegrated dangerously as it hit the wire. Methods for throwing objects safely were found but a backstage drywall that absorbed their impact still had to be repaired daily.

13 During the early 1980s Plaxton was also involved in the renovations to Arts Space in Peterborough, Ontario, and the drawing up of the plans for the changes at the Saidye Bronfman Centre in Montreal.

14 Technical drawings, Theatre Passe Muraille Archives.

15 The footprint for this stage, including the backstage staircases, was 130 feet by 60 feet.

16 Technical drawings, Skylight Theatre Archives.

17 The inclination of these slabs was never extreme, ranging from 5 to 15 degrees.

18 The heights of the towering slabs varied as they encircled the main stone: 9, 4, 8, and 4 feet.

19 Subsequently the theatre decamped to become one of a group of companies resident at Adelaide Court.

20 Soon afterwards the Ice House was renovated to be the du Maurier Theatre at Harbourfront.

21 When it came time to strike the set, chainsaws had to be used to cut up this cardboard structure.

22 Technical drawings, Toronto Free Theatre Archives.

23 Program note, *The Great War* (1992).

24 Marshall McLuhan, *Understanding Media: The Extensions of Man* (Cambridge, MA: MIT Press, 1994), 57.

25 The opening of the first box measured 13 feet high downstage and 9 feet upstage. In his preliminary drawings, Plaxton estimated that 90 sheets of honeycomb cardboard (4 feet × 8 feet × 2 inches) would be sufficient to create the stage. Technical drawings, Theatre Passe Muraille Archives.

26 This worked very well in the tight confines of the Factory Theatre Café where the stage is 20 feet wide, 14 feet high, and 24 feet deep.

27 See Charles W. Jefferys, *The Picture Gallery of Canadian History*, 3 vols. (Toronto: Ryerson Press, 1942–50).

5   Michael Levine

1 In England he designed Stoppard's *Rosencrantz and Guildenstern Are Dead* (Queen's Theatre, Hornchurch, 1983), Moss Hart's *Light Up the Sky* (Old Vic, 1987) and Tourneur's *Revenger's Tragedy* (RSC 1988). His co-designs with Voytek for O'Neill's *Strange Interlude* (Duke of York Theatre, London, and Nederlander Theatre in New York, 1986), were nominated for Olivier and Tony Awards. In Glasgow Levine designed Goethe's *Torquato Tasso*, Goldoni's *The Impressario from Smyrna*, and Beaumont and Fletcher's *The Custom of the Country*, and he returned in 1991 to design Goldoni's *The Housekeeper*.

2 Thornton Wilder's *Skin of Our Teeth* (1984), Shaw's *Heartbreak House* and Clare Booth Luce's *The Women* (1985), Shaw's *Arms and the Man* (1986), and June Havoc's *Marathon 33* (1987).

3 Chekhov's *Uncle Vanya* (1985) and *Designated Mourner* by Wallace Shawn (1997).

4 Wedekind's *Spring Awakening* (1986).

5 Mozart's *Idomeneo* (1987), Berg's *Wozzeck* (1990), *Mario and the Magician* by Harry Somers (1992), *Bluebeard's Castle* by Bela Bartók and *Erwartung* by Arnold Schoenberg (1993), and *Symphony of Psalms* and *Oedipus Rex* by Igor Stravinsky (1997).

6 Their first project, *Mefistofele* by Arrigo Boito, was later remounted by the Lyric Opera of Chicago and the San Francisco Opera. Subsequently they have worked on *Mario and the Magician* by Harry Somers (Canadian Opera Company, 1992), *Regina* by Mark Blitzstein (Scottish Opera, 1990), *A Night at the Chinese Opera* by Judith Weir (Sante Fe, 1989), *I Capuletti e i Motecchi* by Vincenzo Bellini (Geneva Opera/ Opera Bastille, 1990), *A Midsummer Night's Dream* by Benjamin Britten (Le Festival d'Aix en Provence/English National Opera, 1991), *Cendrillon* by Jules Massenet (Welsh National Opera, 1993), *La Bohème* by Giacomo Puccini (Vlaamse Opera, 1994), *Nabucco* by Giuseppe Verdi (Opera Bastille, 1995), *Jerusalem* by Giuseppe Verdi (Vienna State Opera, 1995), *Dialogue of the Carmelites* by Francis Poulenc (The Netherlands Opera, 1997), *Eugene Onegin* by Petr Ilyich Tchaikowsky (Metropolitan Opera, 1997), and *Die Frau Ohne Schatten* by Richard Strauss (Vienna State Opera, 1998).

7 *Tectonic Plates* (du Maurier Theatre at Harbourfront, Toronto, 1988, and tours to Cottesloe Theatre at the National Theatre, London and Tramway, Glasgow); *A Midsummer Night's Dream* by William Shakespeare

(Olivier Theatre at the National Theatre, London, 1992); and the opera double bill *Bluebeard's Castle* by Béla Bartók and *Erwartung* by Arnold Schoenberg (Canadian Opera Company, 1993, and tours to New York [Brooklyn Academy of Music (B.A.M.)], Edinburgh, Geneva, Melbourne, and Hong Kong).

8 Produced by Rhombus Media. Levine won a Gemini Award for Best Production Design.

9 Stravinsky's *Oedipus Rex* and *Symphony of Psalms* (Canadian Opera Company, 1997).

10 *Dr. Ox's Experiment* by Gavin Bryars (English National Opera, 1998).

11 By John Mighton (Theatre Passe Muraille, 1997).

12 By Wallace Shawn (Tarragon Theatre, 1997).

13 Susan Coyne's adaptation of Chekhov's early work (Soulpepper Theatre, 1999).

14 Designs for Stavinsky's *Oedipus Rex* and *Symphony of Psalms* (Canadian Opera Company, 1997).

15 Technical drawings and maquette, Shaw Festival Archives. Selected original costume sketches, Michael Levine Collection, Toronto Public Library.

16 Michael Levine Retrospective, Sketchbook 1, 1985/86–88. York Quay Gallery, Harbourfront Gallery (2000).

17 Technical drawings, Shaw Festival Archives.

18 Original drawings of selected costumes, Michael Levine Collection, Special Collections, Toronto Reference Library; see also Shaw Festival Theatre, *The Pictorial Stage*, 76.

19 Ezra Pound, 'Hugh Selwyn Mauberly.'

20 The full title of the play is *Heartbreak House: A Fantasia in the Russian Manner on English Themes*. Levine's designs hint at Viktor Andreievich Simov's design for the third act of the original production of Chekhov's *The Cherry Orchard* at the Moscow Art Theatre in 1904, for which the interior walls of the house were painted as an orchard.

21 Scott McKowen, 'Heartbreak House,' in Shaw Festival Theatre, *The Pictorial Stage*, 69–70.

22 In 1982 President François Mitterand commissioned the Bastille Opera for state-of-the-art production facilities that would allow a greater number of operas in repertory. To that end, Canadian architect Carlos Ott designed a system whereby fully realized stage sets could be delivered from the rehearsal hall to the mainstage, and stored using a system of tracks and elevators. The dimensions of each of these mobile stages are 6.5 metres by 6.5 metres, fully closed, with a standard freestanding height of 13 metres.

23 Special media effects in the production were created by Laurie-Shawn Borzovoy and the lighting was designed by Robert Thomson. Robert Thomson's lighting reinforced the theme of light as revealing, employing intricate effects to suggest the wholly other worlds behind each door and visible only to Judith. A distinct colour and texture of light filtered through each doorway to play out for the spectator the chilling scenarios of the contents.

6   Ken MacDonald

1 Actor Sheila McCarthy, who has worked extensively in theatre and film in Canada.

2 MacDonald designed at the Belfry for the next three seasons and then started designing in Vancouver. (MacDonald designed another version of *Puttin' on the Ritz* by Irving Berlin, which he had designed in the first season at the Belfry, when Don Shipley directed the work in the first season at the newly acquired Royal George Theatre at the Shaw Festival in 1980. MacDonald's elaborate 30-inch-tall sculptural hats for the dancers in the Ziegfield scene were particularly memorable.)

3 MacDonald was the resident designer at White Rock during the 1982 season and designed four productions.

4 *The Man Who Mistook His Wife for a Hat*, with libretto by Christopher Rawlance and music by Michael Nyman (1993).

5 *Susannah* by Carlisle Floyd (1997).

6 *Tell Me What You Think* and *Two-headed* by Spirit of the West (1995).

7 MacDonald received three Jessies for his work in musical theatre as a composer, musical director, and performer during the 1980s.

8 Some of these toured across the country and others provincially: *Last Call* (1982), *North Shore Live* (1983), *Contagious* (1985), *Cheap Sentimental* (1985), *Simple Folk, Songs of a Generation* (1988). For the *Real People Talking Show*

(1984) MacDonald was a musician only. MacDonald was awarded a Jessie for the composition of *Contagious* and for musical direction and best performer for *Simple Folk*. See Reid Gilbert, ' "And then we saw you fly over here and land!" ' 134–47.

9 *7 Stories* (1989), *Ends of the Earth* (1992), *Vigil* (1993), *Other Schools of Thought: The Cost of Living* (1990), *2B Wut Ur* (1992), *Life Science* (1993), *Lawrence and Holloman* (1998), and *The Necessary Steps* (1991, unpublished).

10 Morris Panych, *Other Schools of Thought* (Vancouver: Talonbooks, 1994), ix–x.

11 Adapted from *The Time Machine*.

12 Reid Gilbert, 'Perspectives on Recent Set Design by Ken MacDonald,' 68.

13 Since the peat moss used for the production was from a garden centre and thus organic, the heat of the theatre lights on the jars containing the moss caused some of the lids to pop. In the context, this release of organic energy into the Tarragon Theatre was decidedly, though unintentionally, ironic.

14 During the spring of 2000 the production toured to the Canadian Stage, Bluma Appel Theatre, National Arts Centre, and Manitoba Theatre Centre.

15 Premiered at the Belfry (1992) and mounted at the Tarragon (1996).

16 Created by Morris Panych and Wendy Gorling with the students of Studio 58 at Langara College (1995). Earlier Morris Panych and Wendy Gorling, with Ken MacDonald as designer, had created two other choreographed performances, *Nocturne* and *Scenes from a Courtroom*, in the small black box theatre at Studio 58. These were production projects set to specific music so that the creators and actors conceived of perform-ances and the design for the set during rehearsals.

17 *Relativity* (1953), *Concave and Convex* (1955), and *Ascending/Descending* (1960), all works that seem to defy gravity and seamlessly bring several perspectives which operate perpendicularly to each other.

7 Teresa Przybylski

1 By Michel Tremblay (Tarragon Theatre, 1998).

2 *To Cry Is not So* (1990), a collective creation by Theatre Smith-Gilmour, with designs by Przybylksi, has been performed over 250 times and toured extensively for over a decade.

3 Her designs for Nightwood Theatre have been highly experimental: for Dilara Ally's *Mango Chutney* in the Music Gallery (1996) Przybylski brought the intricacy of computer circuitry together with the mandala; for Diana Braithwaite's *The Wonder Quartet* (1992) in Nightwood's space on Adelaide Street; and *Harlem Duet* by Djanet Sears (1997) in the Extra Space at the Tarragon.

4 Przybylski was a resident designer for the company for the 1992–3 season and has frequently designed there since then.

5 *The Comedy of Errors* (Tom Patterson Theatre, 1994 and 1995); *Two Gentlemen of Verona* (Festival Theatre, 1998).

6 She designed *Red Emma*, with libretto by playwright Carol Bolt and music by Gary Kulesha in 1995; and *The Emperor of Atlantis* with libretto by poet Petr Kien and music by Victor Ullman in 1997.

7 As the resident designer for the Arbour Theatre for the 1992–3 season, she created a flexible set that contained elements to be used for four productions: Paul Ledoux and David Young's *Fire*, Norm Foster's *Wrong for Each Other*, David Carley's *Ashburnham Duet*, and Drew Hayden Taylor's *The Bootlegger Blues*.

8 The dimensions of the open space in the Tarragon, in the theatre's usual configuration, are 33 feet in width, 28 feet in depth, and a height to the grid of 17.3 feet.

9 The reconfiguration of Przybylski's frames as they moved into fresh positions was designed to destabilize the concept of a proscenium arch parodied on the upstage wall. This feature of a tradition of theatre architec-ture is very heavily implicated in the social world under satiric scrutiny.

10 The work of Otto Dix (1891–1969) and George Grosz (1893–1959) during the 1920s concentrated on scenes of urban life. Characterized as the *neue sachlichkeit*, or new objectivity, their work depicted a recognizable reality that was exaggerated by colour and artistic medium into caricatures of social interaction and sexuality. See Otto Dix's *Die Großstadt* (1928) and *Tänzerin Anita Berber* (1925) and George Grosz's images of Paris and Berlin society of the 1920s such as *Insider and Outsider* (1926) and *Street Scene, Berlin* (1925).

11 This figure drew on the Tattooed Woman of Dada cabarets in a particularly witty manner. Przybylski provided the performer with a padded bodysuit that masked the actor's physique and made the costume into a Dada collage by creating the 'storage' drawers.

12 For *Red Emma* (1995) an opera by Gary Kulesha with libretto by Carol Bolt presented in the du Maurier Theatre at Harbourfront, Przybylski created a two-tiered set: the upper storey consisted of two end panels depicting urban industrialization while the lower portion showed Goldman's study, with a central panel that became a window when it was inverted. Such juxtaposition of interior with exterior views made the implications of Goldman's political and social position all the more immediate.

For *A Christmas Carol* (1994) adapted by Michael O'Brien for Young People's Theatre, Przybylski also intended to 'bring back what was there before' (Teresa Przybylski) and emphasize that the previous function of the theatre was relevant. To do this she left the back wall of the theatre exposed and constructed in front of it a large wooden machine.

13 The concentration camp at Terezin (Theresienstadt) was known for its intense cultural life. Between 1941 and 1944 cabaret and theatre performances as well as concerts were part of the life of the camp. Viktor Ullman composed this opera at Terezin along with many other works. He was moved to Auschwitz before the work was performed.

14 The dimensions of the room are 118 feet 3 inches by 78 feet 1 inch with a height of 37 feet 2 inches.

15 The Hummer Sisters collective and VideoCabaret had been working together creating performance art and video installations since 1976. Prior to the production of *2nd Nature* their work had been performed in venues such as A Space and other galleries, the Cameron House, Theatre Passe Muraille, Lee's Palace, and the Horseshoe Tavern. For a complete listing of the work of VideoCabaret until 1992 see Michael Hollingsworth and Deanne Taylor, 'VideoCabaret Chronology,' 35–44.

16 The Hummers had previously created such incisively feminist works as *Hormone Warzone* (1983), a satirical survey of birth control, and *Dress to Kill* (1984), a tongue-in-cheek installation of video companions. From 1985 to 1989 Deanne Taylor initiated the collaboration between VideoCabaret, Shadowland Repertory Company, and Carnival artists in Trinidad. In *2nd Nature* Deanne Taylor brought together the politics of the earlier shows with the highly narrative structure of the Carnival mas(querade).

17 In 1985 and for the next four years Deanne Taylor was the driving force behind *Island to Island*, a design and performance collaboration between Toronto and Trinidad artists.

18 The choice of colours for the costume was Deanne Taylor's translation of the coding evident in Carnival costumes. See Michèle White, 'VideoCabaret and the Subversion of "Scenography,"' 48.

19 Maristella Roca, *Pinocchio*. In Joyce Doolittle, ed., *YPThree* (Winnipeg: Playwrights Canada Press, 1995).

20 By Carlo Gozzi, produced by Theatre Smith-Gilmour.

21 By Sean Dixon, produced by Theatre Columbus.

SELECTED BIBLIOGRAPHY

A 10th Season Souvenir Collection of Costume Designs from the Stratford Festival. Stratford, ON, 1962.

Adams, Patricia. *Stage Designers of Canada.* Mimeograph. Montreal, 1977.

Aronson, Arnold. 'Postmodern Design.' *Theatre Journal* 43, 1 (March 1991), 1–13

Bachelard, Gaston. *The Poetics of Space.* Trans. Maria Jolas. Boston: Beacon Press, 1964, rpt. 1969.

Beaupré, Therese. ed. *Theatre Design Explorations/Scénographie au Canada.* Exhibition catalogue from Prague Quadrennial Exhibition, 1979. Toronto: Associated Designers of Canada, 1979.

Belzil, Patricia, and Solange Lévesque. *L'Album du Théâtre du Nouveau Monde.* Montreal: Editions Jeu, 1997.

Blau, Herbert. 'Spacing Out in American Theatre.' *Kenyon Review* 15 (Spring 1993), 27–39.

Bouchard, Mario. *L'art de la scène: passé – présent: Scénographie québécoise 1940–1990.* Montréal: Association des Professionels des Arts de la Scène du Québec, 1991.

Bruce, Harry. *Happy Birthday, Dear Neptune: A Tenth Anniversary Historical Sketch.* Halifax: Rothmans of Pall Mall, 1973.

Carson, Neil. *Harlequin in Hogtown.* Toronto: University of Toronto Press, 1995.

Chassay, Jean-François, et al. *L'Album du Théâtre Ubu: Mises en scène de Denis Marleau, 1982–1994.* Montreal: Cahiers de théâtre Jeu / Éditions Lansman, 1994.

Dafoe, Christopher. *Dancing through Time: The First Fifty Years of Canada's Royal Winnipeg Ballet.* Winnipeg: Portage and Main Press, 1990.

Designs for Theatre: Stratford Festival, 1954–1990. Hanover, NH: Hood Museum of Art, in association with the Stratford Shakespearean Festival Foundation of Canada, 1990.

Enquête sur la scénographie québécoise. Special issue *Les Cahiers de théâtre Jeu* 10 (1979).

Ferry, Joan. 'Experience of a Pioneer in Canadian Experimental Theatre.' *Theatre History in Canada/Histoire du théâtre au Canada* 8, I (1987), 59–67.

Freydefont, Marcel, ed. *Le Lieu, la scène, la ville: Dramaturgie, scénographie et architecture à la fin du Xième siècle en Europe.* Special issue *Études théâtrales* 11–12 (1997).

Gallery/Stratford. *From Sketch to Stage.* Stratford, ON: Gallery/Stratford, 1987.

– *Made Glorious: Twenty-Five Years of Design.* Stratford, ON: Gallery/Stratford, 1977.

Gilbert, Reid. '"And then we saw you fly over here and land!": Metadramatic Design in the Stage Work of Morris Panych and Ken MacDonald.' *Theatre History in Canada/ Histoire du théâtre au Canada* 11, 2 (Fall 1990), 134–47.

– '"Disattending the Play": Framing and Frame Breaking.' *Canadian Theatre Review* 70 (Spring 1992), 4–9.

– 'Perspectives on recent set design by Ken MacDonald.' *Canadian Theatre Review* 91 (Summer 1997), 68.

Guthrie, Tyrone. 'Shakespeare at Stratford, Ontario.' *Shakespeare Survey* 8 (1955), 127–31.

Hollingsworth, Michael, and Deanne Taylor. 'VideoCabaret Chronology.' *Canadian Theatre Review* 70 (Spring 1990), 35–44.

Holmes, Katherine. *Celebrating! Twenty-Five Years at the Shaw Festival.* Erin, ON, 1986.

Izenour, George. *Theatre Design.* New Haven: Yale University Press, 1974, rpt. 1996.

Johnston, Denis. *Up the Mainstream: The Rise of Toronto's Alternative Theatres.* Toronto: University of Toronto Press, 1991.

Kareda, Urjo. 'Architect of Dreams.' *Canadian Art* 11, 3 (Fall 1994), 100–7.

Kerr, Mary. 'Mandragola: A Designer's Portfolio.' *Canadian Theatre Review* 2 (Spring 1974), 34–9.

Knowles, Richard Paul. 'Robin Phillips' Strange and Wondrous Dream.' *Theatre History in Canada/ Histoire du Théâtre au Canada* 9, 1 (Spring 1988), 38–58.

L'Espace théâtral: portrait de la création scénographique, 1991–1994. Montreal: Association des professionnels des arts de la scène du Québec, 1994.

La scénographie au Québec. Special issue *L'Annaire théâtral* 11 (1992).

Laporte, Michel, and Mario Bouchard. *L'Espace théâtral: Portrait de la création scénographique 1991–1994.* Montréal: Association des Professionels des Arts de la Scène du Québec, 1994.

Lasker, David. 'Opera by Design.' *Opera Canada* 37 (Summer 1997), 10–13.

Lista, Giovanni. *La Scène moderne.* Arles: Actes Sud, 1997.

Macdonald, Brian. 'The Work of a Designer.' In *Susan Benson Artist/Designer.* Stratford, ON: The Gallery Stratford, 1989.

Mackintosh, Iain. *Architecture, Actor and Audience.* London and New York: Routledge, 1993.

Mitchell, W.J.T. *Iconology: Image, Text, Ideology.* Chicago: University of Chicago Press, 1986.

– 'What do Pictures *Really* Want?' *October* 77 (Summer 1996), 71–82.

Palomino, Mercedes, Guilerma de Andrea, and Serge Turgeon. *Le Théâtre du Rideau Vert: 50 ans à célébrer le théâtre, 1949–1999.* Montreal: Lemeac Éditeur, Inc., 1999.

Panofsky, Erwin. *Perspective as Symbolic Form.* Trans. Christopher S. Wood. New York: Zone Books, 1991.

Perkyns, Richard. *The Neptune Story: Twenty-Five Years in the Life of Leading Canadian Theatre.* Hantsport, Nova Scotia: Lancelot Press, 1989.

Plunkett, Sheila. 'Women Scenographers Astrid Jansen [*sic*] and Mary Kerr.' *Canadian Theatre Review* 70 (Spring 1992), 20–2.

Polieri, Jacques. *Scénographie – Sémiographie.* Paris: Editions Denoël, 1971.

Quin, Michael L. *The Semiotic Stage: Prague School Theater Theory.* New York: Peter Lang, 1995.

Report: Royal Commission on National Development in the Arts, Letters and Sciences 1949–1951. Ottawa: Edmond Clothier, 1951.

Rewa, Natalie. 'Michael Levine: The Process to See.' *Canadian Theatre Review* 97 (Winter 1998), 41–7.

– 'Scenographic Stories: Design in Contemporary Opera Performance.' *Canadian Theatre Review* 96 (Fall 1998), 9–17.

Rischbieter, Henning, ed. *Art and the Stage in the 20th Century: Painters and Sculptors Work for the Theater.* Greenwich, Connecticut: New York Graphic Society, 1968.

Rudakoff, Judith. 'Mary Kerr: In Conversation.' *Toronto Free News* 4, 2 (Winter 1988), 1, 4–5.

Saxton, Nadine, and Katherine Cornell. *Toronto Dance Theatre 1968–1998: Stages in a Journey.* Toronto: Captus Press, 1998.

'Scénographie' and 'Scénographie' suite. Special issues *Les Cahiers de théâtre Jeu* 62 (1992).

Souvenir Costume Designs from the Stratford Festival. Stratford, ON, 1967.

Shaw Festival Theatre. *The Pictorial Stage: Twenty-Five Years of Vision and Design at the Shaw Festival.* Exhibition catalogue. Stratford: Beacon Herald Fine Printing Division, 1986.

Souchotte, Sandra. 'Designing Women: Four Young Designers Color Their Theatrical World.' *Scene Changes* 8, 1 (1980), 8–15.

– 'Toronto's Baby Building Boom.' *Canadian Theatre Review* 21 (1979), 21–46.

Stuart, Ross. 'A Circle without a Centre: The Predicament of Toronto's Theatre Space.' *Canadian Theatre Review* 38 (1983), 18–25.

Svoboda, Joseph. *The Secret of Theatrical Space:* The Memoir of Joseph Svoboda. Ed and trans. J.M. Burian. New York: Applause Theatre Book Publishers, 1993.

Veltrusky, Jiri. 'Theatre in the Corridor: E.F. Burian's production of *Alladine and Palomides*.' *Drama Review* T84 (23, 4) (1979), 67–80.

Vitruvius, Pollio. *Vitruvius: Ten Books on Architecture.* Trans. By Ingrid D. Rowland. New York: Cambridge University Press, 1999.

Von Tiedemann, Cylla. *The Dance Photography of Cylla von Tiedemann.* National Arts Centre: Ottawa, 1991.

Wallace, Robert. 'The Theatrical Designs of Michael Levine.' *Insite* 3, 1 (September 1993), 42–3.

Watts, Allan. 'Sculptured Spaces: Jim Plaxton in Conversation with Allan Watts.' *Canadian Theatre Review* 70 (Spring 1992), 54–9.

White, Michèle. 'VideoCabaret and the Subversion of "Scenography." ' *Canadian Theatre Review* 70 (Spring 1992), 45–9.

Archival Collections

L.W. Conolly Archives, University of Guelph:

Centre Stage
Shaw Festival
Skylight Theatre
Tarragon Theatre
Theatre Passe Muraille
Toronto Free Theatre

Special Collections, Toronto Reference Library:

Susan Benson Designs
Astrid Janson Designs
Mary Kerr Collection
Michael Levine Collection
Teresa Przybylski Designs

Stratford Festival Archives

Canadian Opera Company, Production Records

English National Opera, Production Records

INDEX OF NAMES

Bold print indicates an illustration number in the portfolio section.

INDEX OF THEATRES

For a general overview of the development of theatre in Canada see pp. 123-8.